Eft Tapping For Beginners – A Step
Step By Step Guide

Written By Jenna Jeong

TABLE OF CONTENTS

INTRODUCTION

EFT tapping is something that a lot of people are just now hearing about for the first time, even though it's been around for quite a while now. It has mainly grown by word of mouth, as orthodox medicine and psychology don't have any way to account for it working within their worldview. Nonetheless, EFT tapping has accumulated hundreds of thousands of success stories over the past couple decades, and word about it is finally getting to the average person in the street, and have a lot of questions. If that's you, this book will introduce you to EFT tapping, and let you know what this buzzword is all about.

EFT stands for Emotional Freedom Technique. (You can see why people use the short version of it!) And the tapping part? That refers to how the technique is administered, which is by using your fingers to tap on various body parts, such as the eyebrow, just below the eye socket, the wrist, the chest, the top of the head, etc. Naturally, when most people first hear about this therapy, they're quite skeptical. How in the world could tapping on parts of the body have any effect, let alone a healing one? Well, that's because the body is full of energy, and these are parts of the body which allow us to access and harness that energy. You're no doubt familiar with the healing practice of acupuncture, which seemed strange and "weird" to most people when it first came to the Western countries several decades back. Well, acupuncture works on the very same principles as EFT tapping.

Nowadays, of course, acupuncture is something that millions of people in North America have had done, and lots of them swear by it. Now it's EFT's turn to first shock and astound people when they first hear about such a radically different way of approaching healing, and then to delight and surprise them when they try it for themselves and see just how effective it is. And with it being free and non-invasive, there's really no reason not to try it. You might feel a bit silly the first few times you tap, but after you've seen what it can do, you'll be changing your tune about EFT tapping.

EFT is an energy therapy technique developed by Mr. Gary Craig for releasing mental and emotional energy blocks by tapping on the acupressure points on the body. EFT is based on the discovery statement that the cause of all negative emotions is a disruption in the body's energy systems. These energetic disruptions then create physical manifestations in the body such as chronic pain, rashes, asthma, and migraines as well as mental conditions such as phobias, anxiety, depression, etc.

Most people are familiar with acupuncture, which is based on the same theory, that there are energy channels (meridians) running throughout the body like rivers of energy or energy pipes, and these meridians can become blocked for one reason or another which is like putting a dam on the energy "river". In acupuncture, needles are inserted into the body to release these blockages but in EFT the tip of the fingers are used to gently tap on these special acupressure points while focusing on the problem, to reset the energy system and promote the free flow of energy. The result is improved physical and mental health and well being.

Another great principle that EFT draws upon is the immense power of Love and Forgiveness in healing basically any condition you can think of. The interesting thing is that for many of us the hardest thing may not be forgiving others as one would think, but forgiving ourselves.

EFT often gets results when nothing else will and has been shown to be effective for the following conditions: Pain Management, Addictions, Weight loss, Allergies, Children's Issues, Animals, Vision, Headaches, Panic/Anxiety, Asthma, Trauma, PTSD, Abuse, Depression, Dyslexia, Carpal Tunnel, Anger, ADD-ADHD, Fears/phobias, Eating disorders, OCD, Blood Pressure, Diabetes, Neuropathy, Fear of Flying, Claustrophobia, Agoraphobia, Anorexia/Bulimia, Sports and other Performance.

You can effectively "dissolve" any of the above conditions by finding the underlying emotional block that is causing the physical condition to be held in place. Once you resolve the emotional or energy blockage with EFT, then the physical condition will also disappear.

EFT tapping is a form of psychological acupuncture. The body is an energy system similar to the electricity that comes to your neighborhood. During a thunderstorm, it's common to see your lights flicker. Or even lose power completely if a tree falls on the electric lines. That's a disruption of the energy system.

All emotion you experience is not only experienced in the mind but in the body as well. And any emotion can get "stuck" in the body. Unless you remove that blockage, the energy in your body doesn't flow freely. Just like a downed power line. Until the electric company comes out to fix it, you don't get your power restored.

EFT tapping helps release these emotional blockages and restore your personal power. A thought or emotion or memory can trigger a disruption in the body's energy system.

That disruption can trigger physical or emotional pain. Or it can prevent us from manifesting what we desire.

WHAT IS THE EFT TAPPING TECHNIQUE

The EFT tapping technique is a fairly new modality in the world of alternative health and healing. It's actually been around for a while, but it mainly spread by word of mouth, and news about it just now starting to get out to the broader world. That being said, it should be pointed out that probably 85 percent of people have still never heard of it, or the branch of alternative health that it's a part of, which is energy healing. That's a shame because it would really benefit millions of people to learn how to use the EFT tapping technique.

The technique couldn't be simpler. It simply involves tapping on your body in various areas, such as the wrist, eyebrow, cheekbone, etc., while making certain statements aloud. By doing so, you activate the body's own natural energy system, and you harness and direct it to bring about healing from problems such as phobias, addictions, self-destructive behaviors, etc. Many people have reported profound differences in their lives by employing EFT tapping, and it's not just limited to the above problems. Lots of people have used it for weight loss and allergies, for example. Everything in the universe is made up of energy, including our body. And the energy fields in our bodies have their own wisdom. We only need to tap into (no pun intended.)

4

Does it work for everyone? No; that should be admitted right up front. But what method of healing does work for everybody? But the majority of people who give it a try, find that they experience some level of healing. Many of them report major benefits, such as being cured of alcoholism or phobias that had plagued them for decades. It takes an open mind to try EFT tapping, but everyone should give it a try if they have any problems they've struggled with for years. They just might find the help they've been seeking in the EFT tapping technique.

Some Benefits of Using EFT to Become Emofree

1. EFT tapping is easy to learn, with a track record of amazing results. The process is gentle and highly effective. Most EFT users can release troubling emotions like fear, anxiety, anger, and stress quite quickly. Often, they only need a single application or several days or weeks of tapping compared with months or years of traditional therapy.

2. EFT tapping is flexible. One of the things you will appreciate most is EFT's versatility. When you have mastered this process, it is almost like having superpowers. You will have tools that you can use with almost any challenge.

For instance, if you are going to an important meeting or interview and feel anxious or afraid, you can just sit in your car or duck quickly into the nearest bathroom and do some EFT tapping.

3. It's a non-invasive holistic approach. The EFT Technique addresses your entire system.

What does this mean? True healing addresses every aspect of your being. It considers all of the parts of you and addresses the source of the problem, rather than just relieving the symptoms.

Any emotional disturbance also has a mental, spiritual, and sometimes even a physical component. A holistic approach clears the blockages in all of these areas and this is exactly what happens with EFT tapping.

4. Becoming emofree practically risk-free! EFT does not involve the use of needles, chemicals, or any invasive surgical procedures.

Gary Craig introduced EFT in 1995 and coined the term emofree. He reported in his EFT Training Manual that this method has no material side effects. He arrived at this conclusion, after using the methods for six years working with hundreds of people. The process generally just involves tapping on a short series of points on the face and upper torso.

5. Most individuals experience partial or total relief from the following types of emotions:

- All kinds of fears and phobias

- Anger and frustration

- Negative thinking

- Painful memories and inner child issues

- Self-doubt

- Stress and anxiety

Guilt, grief, confusion and just about any other emotion imaginable, including those yucky, icky and generally awful feelings you can't even find a name for.

EFT tapping can help you to be emofree and move rapidly on your path to success by releasing all types of obstacles. And if you are a holistic professional, you will probably find, as so many others have, that EFT can supercharge your effectiveness.

RELIEVE YOUR TENSION AND STRESS IN MINUTES - WITH EFT TAPPING!

In today's typical modern fast-paced lifestyle, the number of stress people experience can wreak havoc on the body, especially when it is placed under too much stress for far too long. Many people feel they need help with stress levels that have got out of hand. Tension increases and if it is not released through physical activity like our forebears would have experienced, then not only does the physical body suffer but you may also suffer mentally and emotionally as well.

Each of us has 'weak points' in our bodies. When stress is at an unmanageable level things start to go wrong. You may experience increased tension in your neck and back, you may develop headaches, skin complaints such as psoriasis or even stomach ulcers or heart disease. On an emotional level you may feel irritable, anxious, depressed, or suffer from bouts of insomnia.

If you don't have the tools to cope with chronic stress you could find yourself turning to destructive ways of coping such as overeating, smoking, drugs, or alcohol abuse. Escapism is another form of detrimental coping such as watching movies or sexual addiction in order to escape or take your mind off the problem.

So, what can you do?

If you'd like to reduce or eliminate the tension and stress in your life, you now have an exciting new option to explore. This is EFT, short for Emotional Freedom Techniques, a self-help acupressure tapping method with a high success rate.

You could feel calm within minutes! You can actually manage your emotions!

Sounds too good to be true? EFT is publicly endorsed by well-known leaders in healthcare such as Deepak Chopra MD (who says, 'EFT offers great healing benefits'), Jack Canfield, Donna Eden, Joe Vitale, and others.

The EFT technique is a rapid and easy tapping procedure that can allow you to release painful emotions. Such emotions--which present themselves as anxiety, fear, frustrations, stress, among others--block your path to happiness and success. And continuous stress can likewise become damaging to your physical wellbeing.

How EFT tapping Can Help With Stress

Here is where it becomes exciting. First, you must learn how to perform EFT, which is simple. It may sound strange in the beginning, but you'll probably end up being amazed at the comfort it can give you, frequently in just a few moments.

Keys for Relieving Stress with EFT Tapping

1. Get started. Decide that you want to overcome stress and devote yourself to change. Greater understanding can make it easier to find ways to change your life for the better. Your first task is to explore where the stress is coming from and discover ways you can change it.

What are the situations that result in stress? Take note of your answers. Record all of your observations, regardless of seeming importance.

Now, determine that you want to behave in new ways on these kinds of occasions and perform EFT. Review your initial list of responses, and perform some EFT tapping on each item. As you progress with EFT, you will most likely feel a great release as your overall system relaxes.

2. Bring a new sense of calm into your life. The conditions that have caused stress and anxiety previously could repeatedly reappear. This may retrigger feelings of stress if you don't think and behave in new ways.

How can you reduce external sources of stress? If asked "What did you accomplish today," many of us feel required to produce a convincing record of achievements that justify our existence. Often, we are urged on by a strong feeling of duty or worry about what other people think of us.

We need to completely value ourselves and our skills, regardless of what others assume. If this is true for you personally, you can use EFT affirmations to address the challenges of low self-esteem and instability.

How do you respond in situations you cannot possibly alter? How about being stuck in tangled up traffic or hearing someone else gripe about their troubles?

You need to come up with positive techniques to cope with these types of circumstances. What about listening to an enjoyable song or looking out the window? Simple adjustments can work like a charm.

3. Manage small irritations during the day in this exact manner. Do you dislike the idea of getting stuck in a line? How about getting phone calls from telemarketers? Think of more enjoyable behaviors that will help you cope effectively with the onset of stress. This can involve:

- Doing a few rounds of EFT tapping to take yourself into a more positive state.
- Strolling for a few moments in the open air
- Inhaling a few deep breaths and allowing your mind to relax
- Choosing not to let outside situations spoil your mood

'How do you do EFT?'

This technique is rather like acupuncture without the needles, but with vastly more applications. To do EFT, you tap on key meridian energy points on your head and body while you briefly focus with words on one specific problem at a time.

The basic technique takes about 30 seconds to do, and you may repeat it several times. Results often come quickly when your focus is specific.

For example, to start your EFT tapping process you might say, 'Even though I feel tense when I think of _____ ' (something or someone specific), 'I accept myself.'. Even if you feel you don't accept yourself, EFT covers that possibility.

Stress relief achieved by tapping on specific issues is typically permanent

EFT's successes can feel like magic -- but this energy method has sound new science behind it.

EFT does not take the place of competent medical, psychological or psychiatric consultation. It's an apparently simple stress relief aid you can safely add to any healing system you're using.

'What is EFT good for?'

This self-help method has lots of everyday applications for tension and stress arising from any source (try it for a headache). It can also eliminate mental and emotional stress blockages keeping you from achieving your goals.

As well, EFT is also being adopted as a top practice for safe, effective trauma relief, by thousands of healthcare practitioners internationally. Hundreds of U.S. war veterans report having recovered from Post-Traumatic Stress Disorder following private EFT treatment, although there is no official cure for this often life-threatening condition.

Aid workers take EFT into natural disaster areas to help calm traumatized people and hopefully to avoid PTSD for them. The workers teach the method to at-risk groups, for example, to war orphans in Rwanda.

'How can I use EFT for my everyday tension and stress? '

If your workplace, your home or your school are where you might experience tension and stress, you might like to find out how to use EFT to quickly dissolve your uncomfortable reactions: anxiety, anger, helplessness, sadness, fear, resentment, fatigue, overwhelm, and so on.

The ongoing condition of staying stressed can lead to serious health consequences.

Even if your uncomfortable feelings are perfectly justified, hanging on to them becomes a health hazard for you. Today it's well known that a majority of serious diseases are largely connected with stress buildup.

Unfortunately, stress hormones don't care whose fault something is, or how right you are! EFT can take care of that.

'When would I tap?'

You could do a daily stress clear-out that's easy and free, tapping away any emotional upsets and discomforts you feel at that time. You might tap for 5 or 10 minutes a day.

And throughout the day, as you feel anxious or angry about problems that arise, you can immediately tap away new stress.

(Obviously, you will have to find a private place to do your tapping, because although we're now comfortable with mobile phone users chatting and laughing and waving their arms when alone in public, tapping on yourself does look eccentric.

With these ideas, you have a number of effective and useful approaches for using EFT as a stress relief technique and an effective cure for anxiety. Don't forget, you and you alone are in command. Decide to create an enjoyable, stress-free daily life!

HOW TO USE EFT TAPPING WITH THE LAW OF ATTRACTION

Before you even start becoming intentional about shifting your vibration towards alignment with your dream life, you need to be prepared to deal with the resistance that will likely show up. The failure to have these tools to do so is what accounts for virtually all perceived failure of Law of Attraction techniques or programs. ~ Bob Doyle

Since the cause of all perceived failure of desired manifestations is resistance, EFT (Emotional Freedom Technique), also known as tapping, is a perfect match to the Law of Attraction because it literally taps out the resistance that keeps you from having the life you want.

Resistance is anything that is not in harmony with your Inner Being. It comes in the form of negative emotions such as fear, anger, anxiety, depression, and can slow your energy down. Resistance wears you down and over time, manifests physically as illness or pain.

EFT helps to release resistance by balancing the energy system of the body and restoring emotional alignment. This allows the body and mind to resume their natural healing abilities. EFT often works when nothing else will.

EFT is easy to learn and apply. While focusing on an issue you want to release, affirmation and reminder phrases are repeated as you tap various acupressure points on the body with your fingers. Often the process only takes minutes to achieve results. In other cases, it may take a little longer if there are underlying issues that also need to be addressed.

EFT can be used with the Law of Attraction in the following ways:

Negative Emotions - You can use EFT to dilute or eliminate feelings of sadness, anxiety, anger, frustration, jealousy, resentment, or any other negative emotion that lowers your vibration and robs you of your natural state of well-being. EFT is an excellent tool to reduce your stress levels and restore your sense of peace.

Limiting Beliefs - People get hung up on all sorts of limiting beliefs of why they shouldn't, why they can't, what others might think, and beliefs about what might happen if they succeed (example: "It's not safe to succeed.") Tapping out limiting beliefs will help you to break the cycle of self-sabotage so you can be successful at whatever dream or desire you pursue.

Affirmations - After tapping out negative emotions or limiting beliefs, tap in at least a couple rounds of positive phrases, such as "I am worthy of joy," "I am worthy of being happy," "Happiness and joy are my birthrights," "I allow myself to be happy." This has worked exceptionally well with my clients and leaves them feeling uplifted and optimistic.

Visualization - Tapping on the meridians of the body stimulates the energy flow, which allows the mind to be more open and receptive to your input. Tapping in positive statements while visualizing what you want enhances the experience and gives a sense of stronger belief that you can truly have what you are visualizing. You can use statements such as "I see myself winning the lottery! It feels exhilarating to know that I am now financially free and secure." while you are picturing yourself with a winning lottery ticket.

Meditation - Spending time in meditation on a daily basis is highly recommended as a resistance release technique for the Law of Attraction. But if you're like me and have a difficult time quieting your mind, try using EFT before you begin your meditation process. You can use statements such as "Even though it's hard to quiet my mind," "Even though it's difficult to suspend my thoughts for 15 minutes," or "Even though I can't stop thinking." Tapping is very calming and will help you to relax your body and mind for a more satisfying meditation experience.

Although EFT is simple to use and very forgiving, there are a few tips that will help you to achieve optimum results:

Drink water before and after tapping. EFT is more effective when you are hydrated and the water helps to flush out any toxins that are being released from the tapping.

Be consistent. Make tapping a priority and set time aside daily to focus on tapping out any negative stuff you might be dealing with in your life. I like to use EFT after my meditation time. My day always runs smoother when I include it as part of my morning routine.

Be persistent. If you don't get results, keep trying. There may be other aspects to explore and tap on. If a seemingly unrelated thought comes up during a round, tap on it also. There may be a connection that you are not aware of. Ask your Inner Being to guide you.

Relax and have fun! Remember not to take yourself too seriously and keep an open mind.

Having a simple, yet powerful tool like EFT to eliminate your limiting beliefs and negative self-talk will prove to be an essential key for leveraging the Law of Attraction! After you have learned to make EFT a habit and experienced the amazing results of using it with the Law of Attraction, you'll wonder how you ever got by without it. Soon you will be attracting everything you have been wanting into your life.

HANDLING YOUR CHILD'S EMOTIONAL CRISES WITH EFT

When your child comes to you in an uncontrollable fit of anger following an incident at school for example, how do you respond or handle the situation?

Do you get angry yourself? Do you offer reassurance and try to clam your child down with soothing words? Do you listen to their story? Do you try and distract them from their emotions with another activity? Do you try and offer solutions or help them come up with their own? Do you dismiss it because in your eyes they are overacting? Do you feel frustrated and powerless because you don't have a clue about what to do?

These might be some of the ways parents respond to a child who is in the middle of an emotional crisis. As parents who have experienced this scenario would probably know, it can take quite some time to get your child to calm down and furthermore resolve the issue, even with a lot of attention and guidance from you. If left alone to 'work it out', the child might internalize that anger, without having an appropriate means of releasing it. Sometimes parents don't have the time, energy and resources to handle a child in crisis. With EFT as an intervention, your child's emotional crisis can be dealt with at the moment and can be diffused within minutes.

For parents who have not heard of EFT, it is a remarkable energy technique for safely and naturally releasing negative emotions by tapping on various acupressure points on the body and can be used to effectively handle your child's emotional crises and at the same time diffuse and calm your own reactions - making it an empowering method for both children and parents. With the application of EFT, your child's emotional state can be transformed from screaming and yelling, crying or panicking one minute to peaceful, calm and happy the next.

A mother recently told me about her 7 year old daughter who came home from school one day in such a fury over an incident with a boy, that she was not only totally taken aback by her daughter's intense anger and hatred towards the boy, but also at a loss as to how to calm her down. Talking it through simply didn't work and seemed to make her angrier. I spoke to the mother about how EFT could have been used as an intervention to release the anger on the spot and help her daughter to calm down, with a strong chance of even forgetting about the matter altogether. As a parent, this would have saved her many hours of frustration, since nothing she tried would calm her daughter down.

When a child (or adult) is angry, according to EFT theory, what really occurs is a disruption in the body's energy system and clearing the disruption by tapping certain acupressure points brings about instant stress relief. In children, this appears to happen quite rapidly. I have used EFT with both children and adults and marvel at how children resolve their issues far more rapidly. After tapping a few rounds on an issue that is upsetting them, children will often lose the charge surrounding the issue so that it no longer has a strong emotional pull, leaving them free to get on with playing, having fun and enjoying their precious childhood years.

Let's imagine now, that your child has learned to tap for themselves and they approach you in a fit of anger. To help your child calm down you could:

Listen to their story and remind them to start tapping as they continue to tell you about what is upsetting them. Remaining neutral, simply LISTEN (without reaction or judgment) and encourage them to tap until they have finished telling you their story. At the end of their story, ask the question: what is upsetting you most about this now? Continue to listen as the child tells you what is upsetting them most. Within a few minutes of tapping it is likely that the anger they felt before they started tapping has been significantly reduced and all you had to do was listen and remind them to tap.

A child who has been properly skilled up in EFT may in future tap on their own and you might only hear the tail end of the story, after which they tapped on it may not be as dramatic or profound. There are also those cases when children won't talk about what is upsetting them but if they know how to apply EFT themselves they can tap on what is bothering them and release the emotion rather than bottling it up or suppressing it.

Childhood can certainly be a turbulent time but with EFT we can equip children with a simple tool to help them manage their own emotions in times of crisis. Teaching children to tap is not only an excellent way to help them deal with everyday emotional traumas but also prevents the emotional scars of childhood from sticking around until adulthood. In addition, a child who uses EFT every day strengthens their personal resilience and enhances their emotional intelligence.

EFT TAPPING - THE ANSWER TO NATURAL RELIEF FROM PAIN AND EMOTIONAL TRAUMA

What is emotional trauma and can it be healed with EFT Tapping? Firstly, emotional trauma is an event or a series of events which you find incredibly overwhelming such as surviving an earthquake, tsunami, hurricane, tornado, or severe flooding. It can also apply to accidents such as a car crash, plane crash, losing a limb in machinery et cetera. Other examples of emotional trauma are when you've been the victim of, or a witness to serious violent crime such as a robbery, rape, or murder.

It can leave the person feeling absolutely overwhelmed experiencing a wide range of emotions. There will, of course, be the immediate overwhelming feelings that are to be expected but longer term, when emotional trauma, if not dealt with it, can frequently lead to a lifetime of emotional and often physical pain - let us not forget the strong connection between the mind-body! It is not uncommon for a person to find themselves having flashbacks, nightmares, insomnia, heart palpitations, or irrational thinking. They may also find that events in the future lead them to react in ways that even surprise themselves. They might find their anger explode in a rage or feel a sudden welling up of enormous sadness.

With stress and anxiety building in our lives as a result of pressure from the outside world, many people are seeking therapies that can help to bring balance back to the mind and body. EFT tapping is one of the self-help therapies that not only release stress but also benefit the body by resolving physical and/or emotional pain and discomfort. The technique is also known as Meridian Energy Tapping that offers freedom from panic, depression, anger, and addiction. All emotional problems can be cured by practicing this technique.

This tool is quite effective and has been successful in dealing with deep emotional issues, hence this therapy is also denoted as emotional acupuncture that uses no needles. It has proven to be very helpful in dissolving negative patterns and beliefs that hold us back in our personal life, career, and relationships. With a diligent application of the therapy's technique, many emotional ailments can be treated and cured eradicating any need for medication or other treatment.

The tapping therapy involves the use of fingertip tapping on certain points of our body. Basically, the technique has two components. One is tapping on certain locations of the body. The second is the positive affirmations that are stated while tapping. The objective of tapping is to stimulate the acupuncture meridian points present in our body with our fingertips and utilizing their energy to restore our body's balance. The tapping should be done solidly but not forcibly. Remember the objective is to simply stimulate the points to heal the body and not to hurt it. Each point on the body is tapped at least 5 to 7 times or about the length of time, it takes for one full breath. To begin the therapy, it is essential to know the tapping points and their pathway down the body. Also, it is good to know that traditionally the technique used only the index and middle finger of one hand, but now both hands and all fingers can be used as it allows access more to acupuncture points and can cover larger surface area.

To apply the therapy, knowledge of the correct points is vital. To begin the procedure, the top of the head is tapped first. Then moving down the head, tap on the start of the eyebrow. Moving around the eye, tap the side of the eye and then underneath the eye in the center. Now tap the point located at under the nose, roughly midway between the bottom of the nose and the top of the lip. Finishing up the head, tap on the chin. Move to the body and tap the collarbone spots. Then finish up by reaching under the arm and tap on the side of the body. Coupled with this tapping technique always remember to softly or silently say positive affirmations as you move from point to point. For example, you may recite "I am always safe' or "I love myself".

These simple phrases become all-powerful when tapping on the body's energy centers. There are many books filled with examples of positive affirmations. Choose some that make you feel good and try around stating that one affirmation as you tap on each point. An EFT coach can work with your certain issues and build a personalized script for you to recite. There are also examples of EFT scripts online targeting specific issues such as weight loss or smoking. Applying the tapping technique sends out a vibration that resonates throughout your system releasing energy and restoring the mind, body, and soul.

The time has arrived for the internal healing of the body to be performed through emotional restoration therapies like EFT tapping rather than relying on drugs or other medical procedures.

EFT TAPPING CURES EXTREME CHRONIC ACID REFLUX

A lot of you may know that emotional stress often underlies any number of physical pains and illnesses and that if you can find a way to deal with emotional stress, it relieves the physical illness.

I had a client a few years ago-we'll call her Sally who, for 2 years in the recent past, had suffered from severe acid reflux due to irritable bowel disease, so bad that she was hospitalized several times. It had started happening again in the last few months. What would happen is that her stomach would start to burn and then the burning would rise up through her esophagus and throat and, every time, she would end up vomiting. It was extremely painful. This was happening a lot again lately. Doctors had tried several medications but nothing helped. They were out of ideas. Sally was open to EFT Tapping, energy psychology.

EFT Works for Physical Pain and Illnesses

I specialize in a method called EFT-Emotional Freedom Techniques-which is extremely effective with stress, trauma, PTSD and often with physical pain and illnesses. It also works really well for phobias and fears, anxieties, allergies, addictions, weight issues, and physical and emotional after-effects of injuries and accidents.

How EFT Works

Researchers have discovered that physical pain is often the result of stress, which makes sense, because, when our nervous system is stressed or traumatized, one of the ways this manifests is physical pain. For example, our muscles might cramp, our stomach might hurt, we might get headaches or burning feelings, etc. So, if we can calm the nervous system, it often leads to pain disappearing. EFT (Emotional Freedom Techniques) is great for that. We tap on energy meridians (it's like acupuncture without the needles!) while focusing on the emotional pain underlying the physical pain. EFT Tapping is more effective than many other modalities because it also deals with the parts of us that might be afraid of making changes.

Anger-the Underlying Emotional Pain

When she first came in, Sally mentioned that she was going to visit a relative we'll call John, to whom she used to be very close. This person was her best friend and had helped her through the craziness of her family during childhood. But now John was very jealous of her for a number of reasons and so they argued a lot. Sally was angry at John and full of anxiety.

As she was talking about this, her stomach started burning!

We started EFT Tapping, focusing on the anger. The burning lessened, and she noticed that now she was aware she was sad that she couldn't share with John and that she was actually giving up on him. This was a huge loss for her.

Sadness-the Second Underlying Emotional Pain

We did some more EFT Tapping, this time on the sense of sadness and loss around giving up on the relationship. The burning stopped!

She Had Never Been Able to Stop the Burning Once it Started

But this time, it stopped. She felt like things were shifting inside her. She cried because she was so moved that this time, the burning didn't get worse and worse, rise up in her throat, and make her vomit. It just stopped!

Getting to the Emotional Cause Cured Acid Reflux

At a follow-up appointment, Sally said that every time the burning started, she was able to stop it by just beginning EFT Tapping. She didn't even have to go through the whole sequence of tapping. After several times of tapping on her own, the burning never even started again. In a few other sessions, we worked on another physical illness, which was also cured. The acid reflux never came back.

EFT is exceptionally effective energy psychology and alternative therapy, where EFT Tapping on acupuncture meridian pressure points are used to take emotional charge out of traumatic and painful memories and experiences, often alleviating pain.

EFT TAPPING - THE INDISPENSABLE ULTRA-MODERN TOOL

EFT, short for Emotional Freedom Techniques and otherwise known as Tapping, is an acquired taste. It mjght only take you a whole year to try it and you'll be hooked immediately. And different people have different initial feelings about it.

The classical form of EFT uses drumming with the fingers on special acupressure points (tapping), combined with voicing our negative self-talk. The combination is a little like the mythical miracle elixir that cures most ills. Only it is a real method that releases most emotional and many physical conditions. Newcomers to EFT sometimes feel uncomfortable about the idea of tapping looking strange, the thought of voicing negative self-talk rather than try to ignore it, and of course, there is that question of "What if someone saw me tapping and thought I'm going mad?"

Yes, the tapping, being a relatively new method, seems strange at first. It can also initially seem wrong if we are tapping away negative talk. Hence the step by step introduction. But You will soon ease into it and find it a great tool. I remember when the personal computer was invented, and that was before laptops, tablets, and smart-phones. Now, what would we do without computers and our mobile phone?!

Now, mobile phones have an interesting story. I remember when they first came out in the 1980s. They were huge brick sized things. We (showing my age here) used to laugh at the early adopters, thinking they were showing off with their new gadgets. Now, nobody laughs. We need our mobile phones. They keep us in touch with our friends, work, and loved ones. They keep us safe, as we can call emergency services with them or call for roadside assistance if our car breaks down. And they give us train and bus details when we are traveling by public transport. When we take a walk, our mobile phone provides us with a map.

In the same way, the early adopters of EFT were seen as strange and EFT, even at the time of writing this book, is seen as comical or silly by many people. And yet the same people often come back to using EFT and wonder how they ever coped without it!

Put it this way, is it sillier for someone to tap for a few sessions or to always be seen with nails bitten down to the quick? Is it sillier to tap for period pain or a debilitating backache or to suffer in pain or take lots of painkillers instead? After all, pills are rarely without side-effects. And pain, well, I'd tap instead any day.

EFT Tapping - 15 Points of Power

The most important part of learning proper EFT tapping is getting a powerful sequence of tapping points mastered to the level of habit.

You want to be able to go through the tapping sequence without having to think about the points. This frees up your mind to focus on the issue and the desired outcome.

Once you habitually know a sequence of points, you can quickly use EFT tapping to resolve a wide variety of mental, emotional, and even physical problems.

This is a list of some of the most common and easy to find EFT tapping points:

The Crown Point: The center of the top of your head. Use 4 fingertips of one hand (or both hands) to tap.

The Eyebrow Point: The inside edge of both eyebrows right next to the nose. Use 2 or 3 fingertips to tap.

The Outer Eye Point: On the orbital bone on the outside of either eye. Use 2 or 3 fingertips to tap.

The Under Eye Point: On the orbital bone beneath either eye. Use 2 or 3 fingertips to tap.

Beneath the Nose: Just below the nose at the top of the upper life. Use 2 or 3 fingertips to tap.

Beneath the Mouth: Just below the lower lip and above the point of the chin. Use 2 or 3 fingertips to tap.

Beneath the Collar bone: About one inch directly below the inside point of either collar bone. Use 2 or 3 fingertips to tap.

Beneath the nipple: Just beneath the nipple for men and just beneath the breast for women. Use 2 or 3 fingertips to tap.

Underneath the arm: Roughly 4 inches below the armpit on either side. Use 4 fingertips to tap.

Thymus: The center of the sternum. Use 4 fingertips to tap.

Side of the thumb: Use 1 finger to tap the side of the thumb. The point is in line with the base of the fingernail.

Important Note: If you look at the back of your left hand, all of the finger points are on the right side of the fingers. If you look at the back of the right hand, all the finger points are on the left side of the fingers.

Side of index finger: The same as the thumb, only located on the index finger.

Side of middle finger: The same as the thumb, only located on the middle finger.

Side of ring finger: The same as the thumb, only located on the ring finger.

Side of little finger: The same as the thumb, only located on the little finger.

Spend a few seconds tapping each point while breathing deeply. 5 to 7 taps per point will work if you would like to use a specific number. You will eventually start to do it by feel. You will intuit which points need more attention, and you might notice some points need no tapping at all.

If you tap these 15 power points regularly while focusing on your challenges or your goals, you will quickly overcome the challenges, you will start to achieve your outcomes much more easily, and you will vastly improve your satisfaction with life.

WHAT EFT TAPPING IS AND WHAT IT IS NOT

Every now and then, there is controversy about what constitutes EFT Tapping, EFT, or Tapping, and what does not. It can be very confusing if you are looking to learn EFT or thinking of using an EFT practitioner. With this in mind, here are a few pointers about what constitutes EFT, Tapping, or EFT Tapping (The distinction will become clear).

Every form of EFT has these elements in common:

It is an energy healing modality. Although often called "Energy Psychology", it is as far removed from psychology as any other energy modality, such as Reiki, Spiritual Healing, and Kinesiology, to name but three of many. In other words, when we do EFT, we do not do a great deal of counseling, NLP, or psychotherapy. We do energy work to release blocks in our path to emotional and/or physical wellbeing.

It gently brings up a specific energy disruption to the surface, and then specifically directs the energy in such a way as to release this disruption. This is where Optimal EFT differs from other kinds. Other kinds use Tapping on the meridian end-points to achieve the release. This includes Classical, Gold Standard, and Energy EFT, for example. Optimal EFT directs the energy as if channeling energy via Spiritual Healing or Reiki rather than by tapping with the fingers on the meridian end-points, with the difference that it directs the energy very specifically at the exact problem to be released.

It is very specific. For example, we can work on releasing that pain in our shoulder on the top right near where it meets the neck, or the time when a teacher gave us a fail when we were 9 years old, or the need to feel more in control when facing a certain authority figure, We get as specific as we can, to pull the problem at the root.

It is gentle. There is no point dwelling incessantly on the past, forcing ourselves to face our fears, learning to cope with tragic circumstances, accepting living forever with progressive disease and giving in to a perceived fate, or anything like that. Rather, the user has hope and does not go anywhere they feel uncomfortable.

It involves a readiness to let go with peace and calm, using a calming start or a calming implication as soon as the process starts. It is not a method of mind control or even a method of mind persuasion, such as hypnotherapy. And unlike hypnotherapy or hypnosis, you do not need to believe in EFT for it to work. It involves a safe space where you can feel free to let go of the energy disruptions behind your challenges.

LEARN ABOUT THESE TIPS BEFORE YOU TAP:

1. Drink a full glass of water before tapping to stimulate and prepare your body's electrical system

2. You can tap down either side of your body with either or even both hands, or try alternating

3. Don't tap too hard. Use the same amount of pressure you would as if you were drumming your fingers on a table.

4. Take a slow deep breath after you complete a round of tapping to help move the energy through your body

5. Yawning during tapping is a sign that you are releasing energy, so let out the yawns and keep going

6. When you tap along with a group of others (either live or via recording), you will experience "borrowing benefits" whether or not you are the "primary tapper". So always tap along.

7. The key to tapping is to "tune in" and always ask yourself "How does this make me feel?" and that will be your guide.

It's actually common for people to have anxiety about not knowing what to say when they tap for themselves. The good news is - there isn't a wrong way to do EFT, you can't make a mistake or hurt yourself.

If you're having issues about knowing what to say, then choose from these powerful EFT affirmation phrases to help you move forward. These examples were drawn from actual EFT tutorials given by several of the top EFT practitioners in the field.

Here's a list of the most powerful EFT affirmation phrases to use while tapping:

You can say things like: I choose to, I prefer to, I intend to, I decided to, I embrace, I love feeling, I allow myself to, I am grateful for, what if I could, I wonder if, I'm considering, and wouldn't it be fun if.

And you can mix and match these positive affirmations with one of these many helpful phrases

I love and accept myself anyway

I forgive myself for feeling

I know I did the best that I could

I accept things just as they are

I am okay with where I am NOW

I feel safe

I am at peace

I feel powerful

I am inspired

I feel calm and confident

I trust my inner guidance

I release the need to

I let go of the guilt,

I let go of the shame

I let go of the resentment

I let go of the fear

Some people get bored repeating the typical "I deeply and completely love and accept myself" affirmation. This mix of EFT phrases can help to stimulate a more specific reaction and better clearing. Play around with them and add your own words.

As always, to get the best results with EFT, tune into your feelings and intuition and let them guide you. Of course, if you're still having trouble clearing your limiting beliefs on your own, then visit an EFT practitioner because this technique works for everyone and you just might need a little extra guidance.

DOES EFT TAPPING WORK FOR CHILDREN?

Every living thing has energy flowing through it. This is why Emotional Freedom Techniques work on children, middle-aged individuals, those over 50, and even animals. You may have heard of the negative side effects associated with medication prescribed for Attention Deficit Disorder (ADD) in children.

EFT can be used successfully for treating ADD in kids, with no side effects. There are no drugs or doctors involved. This calming, stress-relieving activity understands that emotional issues cause very real physical and mental health conditions. Sometimes children don't even understand why they feel the way they do.

They just know that their emotions are "out of whack". They act out, find it hard to pay attention and feel out of control. The negative emotions which lead to these behaviors arise from an imbalanced energy state. When energy cannot flow properly, it can build up in unhealthy levels. It also becomes weaker. Tapping very specific energy "highways" in a child's body gets this energy flowing properly again.

This leads to emotional control and calming relief for children, and also works on adults. Positive and negative health, mental and emotional, spiritual and physical, have to do with your energy flow. A tapping practice keeps your energy moving properly, and is effective in children and adults to treat a number of conditions.

5 Things You Must Know Before Doing EFT With Children and Teens

Tapping with children can be a very rewarding experience. In many cases, children take to tapping much faster than adults because they are more willing to try new things and aren't hung up on why something is working. They just want to feel better.

Here are five things to keep in mind when teaching kids to tap. (Note: All five lessons below are hard won. I know them to be true because I have done the opposite of all 5 at one point.)

1) They Are Smarter Than You Think

I recently spoke to 600 middle school students about bullying. To start the presentation I talked about why bullies bully. I talked about what happens on an emotional level and how that affects our choices. At the end of the presentation, the children broke up into small groups with their adults to talk about what they can do to stop bullying in their schools. After the small group time, a number of the adults walked up to me to express how surprised they were with the complexity of thoughts the kids had, the emotions they experienced, and how overall thoughtful they were.

Kids don't have the vocabulary to express their emotions and thoughts the way adults do, but they are thinking real thoughts about their lives, their emotions, and who they are. Give them space to talk about their emotions, teach them how to talk about them, and they will surprise you (in really good ways).

2) You Must Be Authentic Or They Will Tune You Out

Kids today are very savvy because of their access to information and technology. They are treated by big business as a market place and they are constantly sold to through TV and online. Because of this, they have very sophisticated BS detectors and they can tell when someone is not being authentic with them.

It is very tempting to want to be cool and hip when talking with kids (especially teens), thinking you are "speaking their language". It is just the opposite. They don't want some line or for you to talk like them. They want someone who is just being who they are, even if that means being your dorky self.

You can't ask a child to honest with their emotions and be comfortable inside their own skin unless you are willing to try to do the same.

3) Your Job Is To Love Them; Not Be Loved By Them

When we are working with teens or children we are doing it because we want better for them. That is the goal. Nothing more. Nothing less. We are not trying to be their friend and we are not trying to gain their admiration. We have our own friends and peers for that. This doesn't mean that we act like jerks or that we don't care, forgetting to treat them with respect. Sometimes wanting the best for someone is asking them to do difficult things and things they might not enjoy.

To help them heal we need their respect, not their love and affection. It is ok to be comfortable with that notion.

4) Teach Them Tools

Children (and most people) don't care how or why tapping works. They are just looking for something that makes them feel better. When working with kids and teens give them tools. They don't need theory. They want to be better, happier, and healthier. Once they know the tool works they might ask you how it works and why.

I love coming up with little processes that are easy to follow.

For example, a great way for parents to teach kids to tap for themselves is to have them tap and explain four things whilst they are tapping.

- What was the best part of the day?
- What was the worst part of the day?
- What are they looking forward to tomorrow?
- What are they worried about tomorrow?

Very simple. It is easy to remember and easy to do. Once they have the tools they can take care of themselves.

5) Start With How The Emotions Feel In The Body

As I said above, children (and many adults) don't have the skill or vocabulary to talk about their emotions as emotions. I like to have them talk about how the emotions feel in the body to help them to tune in.

They might not have the vocabulary to talk about the disappointment that comes with poor grades vs. fighting with a friend. They might call both of these emotions "mad". But if you get them to talk about how it feels in the body they will be able to be more specific. By describing where the emotion is in the body (head, hands, stomach...) and how it feels in these places (heavy, tight, hot...) they will be much more successful with their tapping.

Go For It

You don't have to be perfect when working with teens or children. They are looking for adults who care about them and care about their well being. Show up from a place of love, treat them with respect, and be ready for lots of questions and you will be a great tapping teacher and tapping role model for them.

EFT AND INSOMNIA: HOW EFT TAPPING CAN HELP YOU GET A GOOD NIGHT'S SLEEP

When you're lying sleepless in your bed at night, do you dream of a weekend away at a spa so you can relax enough to sleep peacefully for eight to ten hours at a stretch? Unfortunately, most of us don't have the time or money to go off to a spa every weekend. EFT (Emotional Freedom Techniques) can help.

EFT tapping is a meridian tapping system that can help with insomnia and the factors contributing to it, like anxiety, stress, pain or anger.

Meridian tapping system? Huh?

In ancient China, practitioners discovered places in the body where, when a needle or pressure was applied, this tended to help people with various ailments. EFT tapping uses these same places on the face and upper body while "tuning in" to the problem to help release tension, trauma, anxiety, worry and even the causes of sleeplessness.

If you think meridians are just a figment of some very odd people's imaginations, consider this: the British National Health Service (NHS) is now offering acupuncture for certain conditions, like a backache. The NHS doesn't offer treatments that they know don't work.

In addition, research has shown that places on the skin where the ancient Chinese mapped the meridian points show electrical conductivity that is different from other places on the skin.

While tapping on these meridian points on the face and upper body, at the same time thinking about not being able to sleep, or about the anxiety that is keeping you awake, your system releases everything that gets in the way of you relaxing enough to fall into a deep, peaceful sleep.

Most practitioners have anecdotal evidence that it often takes no more than a few minutes of tapping to relax enough to overcome insomnia. Too good to be true? Not really. Most people have the odd sleepless night through worry about something going on at work, money issues or relationship problems. A couple of rounds of EFT can calm those enough to ensure relaxation.

However, some people are real insomniacs, which is a chronic condition of not being physically able to sleep no matter how much you want to. With the help of a skilled practitioner asking intelligent questions, people will often remember their insomnia started about the time of a specific event or series of events at a significant point in their lives. The remaining emotion from those events can be addressed with EFT, bringing about restful sleep for the first time in many years.

How will EFT relax me?'

EFT's amazing success record around the world since the mid-1990s is due to only one thing: the technique gets its results by clearing out disruptions from your meridian energy system. So it's safe to use.

Your meridian system is the same electromagnetic body system that acupuncture works through. However, with EFT you can address a multitude more of life's problems, with a high probability of clearing them away.

You can learn to tap away stress from emotional and/or attitudinal difficulties, mental worries, even body discomforts (try it for a headache).

One at a time, these can all respond to the same 30-second practice, which you may repeat or apply in various ways. Serious difficulties take more time, but you can enjoy successes along the way. You can also have qualified EFT practitioner help by phone or Skype or in person.

I always have a lot of body tension'

Stella was always tense in her neck and shoulders and had been for years. She believed this was because she worked for hours at a computer. She could turn her head only so far to each side.

She had become so used to this discomfort, pain, and stiffness that she thought of this condition as normal - even when relaxing with her feet up.

However, when she visited me (I am an EFT practitioner) I showed her how to tap away the tensions of years - in minutes. The pain and stiffness dissolved in a few minutes.

Now she herself can tap away any discomfort during or at the end of each working day, and enjoy relaxed shoulders.

In turn, this relaxes the top half of her body and so is likely to forestall further body troubles caused by compression... as well as forestalling ongoing expenses for massage and adjustment.

(Many body therapists are adding some EFT skills to their own skills.)

More than a quick fix

Actually, EFT is more than a quick-fix relaxation tool. As an energy method healing aid, EFT de-stresses the energy structures that underlie discord in mind, body and heart feelings. So it eliminates suffering from many sources.

CAN EFT HEAL LONG-TERM DEPRESSION CAUSED BY GRIEF?

Depression can affect people in varying degrees and can range from feeling like one has the blues through to more serious moderate and severe depression. Depression affects a person's thoughts and therefore their feelings and subsequently their behavior. Help for depression usually begins with a look at the symptoms so a diagnosis can be given by a qualified health professional.

When someone you love deeply dies or leaves, the grief and loss is wrenching. You can't imagine how to go on, how to want to go on, how your life can continue without the one you loved. Grief can go on for months or even years, sometimes with little relief. An alternative therapy, or "energy psychology," called EFT (Emotional Freedom Techniques), can bring emotional freedom.

Prolonged grief can be a kind of Posttraumatic Stress (PTSD)

PTSD is what happens when we perceive our well-being is hugely threatened or when we think we might die. Our nervous system moves into a stress or trauma state, and various emotional and physical symptoms automatically result. You can probably see that when a person we love dies, or leaves, at least a part of us would feel a huge threat to our well-being and maybe even to our ability to stay alive. Although intellectually this may not be the case, emotionally, it IS.

Grief is a Complex of Emotions

First, it's important to become aware of all the different feelings and thoughts that make up grief-it's usually not just one feeling, but a complex of emotions:

Sorrow

Loss

Several kinds of fear

Guilt

Anger

Depression (if grief is chronic, and doesn't change quality over time)

There are ways to overcome this huge grief and loss.

Grief is, of course, "normal." Most of the emotions above are normal. But if they continue on without changing or lessening over time, something has gotten stuck in us. That's, again, what PTSD is. Our system is not able to process the huge loss; the result is physical and emotional symptoms that just keep looping and don't work themselves through.

EFT (Emotional Freedom Techniques)

Grief Counseling can be useful. Individuals discovered EFT (Emotional Freedom Techniques) and was hugely impressed with how quickly it works to help people process this stuck kind of grief-an emotional trauma-and to move on with their lives with "emotional freedom." Among other anxiety treatments, EFT is a method whose premise is similar to acupuncture's-when something is perceived as scary, painful or threatening, our energy system is "zapped" and the result is either "negative" emotions, physical pains and illnesses, phobias, anxieties, or other problematic symptoms. This affects our nervous systems and our bodies. EFT helps to balance the energy system and calm the nervous system. Among other issues, what makes EFT more effective as a depression cure than many other methods is that, in addition to tapping on energy meridians, EFT also deals with our unconscious inner resistances to making changes. For instance, even though we may consciously intend to get over chronic grief, something in us is hesitant or afraid to. EFT deals with that hesitancy so that our whole self is ready to heal from emotional pain or physical pain.

What we do with EFT is to tap on acupuncture meridians while saying aloud the experience the client is having. As we tap, emotions, thoughts and body feelings appear, move through and dissipate. As one dissipates, another rises up until, finally, the whole experience is worked through and the person feels relieved of the emotional pain they've been going through. The whole experience is healed.

EFT Case Study Healing Grief

I have worked with a number of people who had such deep, huge long-lasting grief. I'll tell you the story of one of them (name and biographical details changed for confidentiality) and how I worked with him to overcome his deep sense of loss and to move on with his life.

"Jonathan" came to see me a year after he and his wife divorced-she had left him after 10 years of marriage. For over a year, he had been so filled with grief that he had become severely depressed and could barely go to his job. Friends worried about him. He had a hard time doing anything and felt a chronic heavy oppressive sadness.

First EFT Tapping Session

The first emotion that came up was a huge feeling of loss. He and his ex-wife had been together so long; she was his best friend; they did so many things together. We tapped on his broken heart and his belief that he would never get over the sense of loss.

The second thing that arose was the feeling that their drifting apart was his fault because he hadn't confronted her when she started distancing herself from him. As a result of tapping on this, he realized that maybe her distancing was not about him, and that, at that point, she was already gone emotionally and was just acting it out.

He felt that he was like a zombie; that he was dead but still moving and, if it were up to him, he wouldn't move at all because it was just too hard. (This is a feeling that often comes up when people are grieving).We tapped on all of that and he started to feel that he could be open to the possibility of life springing up inside him again. He didn't feel it yet, but he was open to the possibility.

Good progress in the first session of EFT Tapping!

Second EFT Tapping Session:

At the beginning of the second psychotherapy session, Jonathan said he felt somewhat better than he had for the last year.

The first theme that came up this time was not being able to understand why his ex-wife stopped loving him. He had thought they were made for each other. They shared so many interests and he felt they were like twins. It was like a part of him was literally torn away. When talked about this, his stomach knotted up and his shoulders became very tense. We tapped on the deep confusion, almost like an existential confusion-how could this happen when it seems we were meant for each other? His shoulders and stomach relaxed and he realized he was open to feeling whole again.

Then a feeling of betrayal arose. His ex-wife had actually started an affair sometime before she ended the relationship with him. He realized that he had seen their love as something sacred and he felt that if the person he loved and trusted most in his life had betrayed him, how could he ever trust anyone else? After we tapped on that deep sense of betrayal and the heartbreak and sadness, he felt open to having the broken trust be healed.

Next arose a deep sadness, a huge feeling of loneliness, a feeling that part of him had been ripped out. He had thought his ex-wife was his "one true love" and now she was gone. If he was wrong about that, how could he ever trust himself to know if he is right or not? It didn't make sense to him that he'd thought someone was his one true love and then she left. As we tapped, a question arose: "Could my one true love still be out there?" A hopeful sign!

He realized that he might be in the process of making a vow never to love again. This is something that many people do. As we tapped, he realized "this may not be too smart" because, surely, if he made such a vow, he certainly never would love

45

or be loved again, whereas, if he was open to it, maybe he could again find love.

Third EFT Tapping Session

At the beginning of this EFT session, Jonathan said he felt even better than before the last session and was going to talk with his doctor about decreasing the anti-depressant medication he had been taking for a number of months. Although he still felt guilty for not noticing that his ex-wife had been unhappy, the guilt was way down from before.

He still felt a sense of loss-he had loved doing things for her and sharing with her. When she started sharing less with him and withdrawing from him, he became scared and insecure. We tapped on these feelings, and they abated.

Then he realized that a part of him didn't want to move on, because, in this part of his mind, that would mean that they hadn't ever had a great love. (This comes up often when people are grieving the loss of a loved one). He felt that the relationship might never have been as good as he thought it was, and, again, he didn't know how he could trust his feelings. Through EFT tapping, the realization came to him that he knew he loved her and that was still true. Even though "love didn't conquer all," maybe he could be open to a new feeling full of light and "awesome love."

After this, he felt the void of not having his ex-wife in his life, of not being able to go home anymore, to her. He felt disposable because she had replaced him. He felt he was living in a nightmare alternate reality and couldn't find his way out of it. Tapping on this alleviated the intensity of all of these thoughts and emotions.

Finally, he realized that a part of him was holding onto the grief because this part felt that letting go of it would mean he didn't love her as much as he thought. This part felt that he should feel so bad that he would die. During our EFT tapping on this belief, it transformed to a feeling that maybe this kind of love would be a selfish love and a generous love would be letting his ex-wife go and to totally accept her for what she had become.

Fourth EFT Tapping Session

Our last session seemed kind of like a "clean-up" session, clearing out what was left over from feelings we had mostly cleared previously. The intensity of feelings was, for the most part, much lower than in the previous sessions-except for anger, which hadn't arisen until now.

There now arose in Jonathan huge anger at his ex-wife for being heartless and cruel. When we tapped a few moments on this, anger transformed to hurt. A bit of the feeling of being disposable (from EFT session #3) came up again and quickly disappeared entirely.

Now came a feeling of disappointment in his ex-wife for how she moved through the process of ending their marriage-she started an affair rather than let him know she was withdrawing from him emotionally, she became cold and distant, etc. He felt abandoned and betrayed. None of these feelings were anywhere near as intense as in previous EFT sessions, and a few moments of tapping reduced each of them to nothing.

He then felt that he had wasted a decade of his life in the marriage, and felt the loss of those years. He suddenly realized he was disappointed in himself for thinking that she could make his love a lie. As we tapped, he realized that no one can do that, that his love was real all along.

At that point, he laughed a bit. "I think I was a bit of a slow learner. I thought I could make someone happy who was not happy with herself." He breathed a huge sigh of relief and realized he felt totally fine. His year-long grief had dissolved and he was ready to move into his new life with joy. After four EFT sessions, we were done!

EFT TAPPING - A PASSPORT TO EMOTIONAL FREEDOM AND STRESS RELIEF FOR ABUSE SURVIVORS

Emotional Freedom Technique or EFT for short is a stress relief method that was created in the 1990s by Stanford Engineer and Peak Performance Coach, Gary Craig. EFT is often described as a psychological needle-free ouchless version of acupuncture.

Ancient Healing Art of Acupuncture: The Source of EFT's Humble Beginnings

Acupuncture is the 5000-year-old science invented by the ancient Chinese. They were the first to research and discover the presence of a network of channels of electrically charged energy particles throughout the body. Today advances in the field of modern science and the emerging field of mind/body medicine continue to demonstrate evidence that our bodies are a low-level electro-magnetically charged system and by harnessing the power of our thoughts we can either create health or manifest illness in our bodies.

Acupuncturists say there are circuits in our body where these floating bits of electrically charged energy particles are constantly passing along and traveling. When these channels of energy, also called meridians get blocked up and congested by our emotional conflicts, fears and negative beliefs we experience mental, emotional, physical discomfort and pain.

$E=MC^2$: The Science Behind EFT

The founding principle of Emotional Freedom Technique is based on Einstein's discovery that $E=MC^2$, which simply stated means that everything is composed of energy. A desk, chair, your house, your breasts, even your thoughts, and memories are all made up of particles of floating bits of energy. This is best known asThe Energy Model which explains that energy can neither be created nor destroyed, it can only be changed.

Gary Craig - *"The Cause of All Negative Emotions is a Disruption in the Body's Energy System."*

Scientists in the field of mind/body medicine are only now just beginning to understand the degree to which our bodies are complex and capable. Like two sides of the same coin, your mind and body are connected. This means that your emotions, thoughts, and beliefs ultimately determine your health. When your energy is flowing freely, you feel good. And when your energy is blocked, you feel terrible.

Founder of EFT, Gary Craig says, "the cause of all negative emotions is a disruption in the body's energy system. This means that whenever you experience pain, disease, cravings, urges, obsessive thoughts, or any negative emotion, the underlying cause is a block in your energy system. In order to clear the distortions that are the source of the negative emotions in your body, EFT works on the basis of tuning into the problem while at the same time gently tapping with your fingertips on different 'comfort spots' on your body.

These are the endpoints of the blocked meridians. By using this gentle tapping motion, it is possible to activate a flooding effect that relaxes muscles, releases stored toxins and initiates a chain reaction of chemical and neurological changes throughout the body. Think of this tapping technique as giving you the power to wipe your mental and emotional slate clean and start over.

The Importance of Changing Your Story

What stories are you telling yourself? What things have you been saying to your body? What feelings do you get every time you look in the mirror?

Most people are pretty hard on themselves, but those who have encountered abuse in their past are extremely self-critical and abusive of themselves, forever pointing out their flaws, putting themselves down, and doubting their own self-worth. These nasty things you say to yourself aren't just in your head. As science continues to prove, your thoughts are energy - an integral part of the universe - each with their own ability to affect the world, and most important, you. Every day your thoughts are creating your reality. It's the Law of

Attraction. Thoughts are tangible, they are energy, and they are constantly moving and vibrating, seeking out thoughts and things of similar vibration. Everything is vibration! What are you vibrating? What are you attracting into your life by the stories you tell and the thoughts you think?

Imagine that the stories we tell ourselves are like a broken record, continuously playing over and over again, in a loop without ever stopping. This is what happens every time you're reminded of an emotionally charged event. Because your brain can't tell the difference between an imagined thought and reality, your body responds as though you're actually re-experiencing the event all over again. If the experience was traumatic and painful, as much as you may want to change and get out of being a victim and feeling helpless, you can't because you're stuck in a rut, unable to move beyond thinking about the problem.

A POWERFUL, PERSONAL EXPERIENCE WITH EFT: LIFE CHANGING STORY

For years as a woman who has endured a history of being sexually abused and verbally battered, I always felt as though I was cursed in life. I acted like and thought of myself as a victim which kept me stuck in so many ways, playing small and being afraid. I was stuck in my life.

Today I credit EFT for healing me. It's given me the most powerful tool I know to transform my fearful and negative thinking, tame my nasty inner critic and make me whole again after being broken and feeling so painfully unworthy for so many years.

Despite being able to function at a high level running a successful multi-million dollar business, I was really living in a private hell, stuck under a dark cloud of fear and shame. Whenever I wasn't working I retreated from the world, just clammed up, hidden away by eating myself into oblivion. Because I felt so horrible about myself and was completely ashamed of my body, I tried to be as invisible as I could be. I avoided most social gatherings. I didn't play full out, I rarely ventured beyond my comfort zone and I never felt safe taking risks. Because I had a basic mistrust of men, I always felt intimidated by them. From the bedroom to the boardroom, I was overly cautious and fearful of expressing myself, saying what was on my mind, standing in my power and letting people know that I had needs and opinions.

Despite somehow finding and marrying a wonderful husband who adores me, I struggled desperately with trust issues. I pretty much kept my heart tucked away, always trying to keep myself safe. Because I had so many negative charged memories around the issue of sex, I didn't feel comfortable loving or being loved. Every fear of the unknown had the potential power to plunge me back into the depths of the darkness of my soul. With insecurity as my constant companion, I was always wondering when the next shoe was going to drop.

It seemed like there were a million situations in life that triggered my fears and pain, constantly threatening my peace of mind and sanity. I could be fine one moment and broken down in tears the next completely swept away by my own fears and imagined horrible circumstances. In a desperate attempt to reconcile and move beyond my many memories of abuse, I spent 18 1/2 years in traditional therapy, with little to show for it.

The day a colleague of mine introduced me to EFT, my whole life changed. At the time, I was experiencing a panic attack, because something I saw and heard in a classroom setting had triggered a memory of sexual abuse that I had experienced in my past. I remember feeling and seeing my body begin to shake uncontrollably as I looked down and watched my trembling hands, vibrating as they bounced on my quivering knees. I could feel the all too familiar lump in my throat and the tension in my eyes as they began to fill with tears. My colleague quickly came to my assistance and escorted me out of the room. As soon as the door closed behind us, my silent tears gave way to heaving sobs.

Within just a couple of minutes of tapping, the emotional charge of the flood of fearful memories plaguing me that day was completely neutralized. Today I still have those same types of memories but I don't feel anything when I think about them. That one single experience that I had with EFT created such an enormous momentum of change in my life that day. For the first time ever, I finally understood that by being unwilling to forgive my abusers and holding onto that anger and hatred, I was only hurting myself. That day forgiveness became a no brainer and I finally realized that forgiveness is a gift you give yourself. With that new insight, I have freed from my self imposed prison of being a victim.

Thanks to EFT, now I am the Juicy Woman. I can see things differently. I can see that painful experience of my abuse as something that, although it was horrible, it was really a powerful learning experience for me because I now realize how strong I am. I know that I would never have the depth of compassion for myself or others if I would not have experienced the abuse I did. Since that first encounter with EFT, I've resolved to share this gift with other women whose lives have also been touched by abuse.

Today I continue to use EFT often and always, whenever a negative memory or fear pops up, I know that I can easily disarm it and glide past it. I consider EFT my recipe for courage in a bottle. My experience of healing with EFT is just one of many thousands of people whose lives have been changed by this simple, silly looking little powerhouse of a technique.

Uses for EFT

You can use the Emotional Freedom Technique to get relief for issues of anger, sadness, fear, shame, overwhelm. It's used to help people to release and neutralize traumatic memories of war, rape, abuse, molestation, eliminate or alleviate physical pain. It works to eliminate all forms of performance anxiety, including fear of public speaking, heights, vertigo, overcome mental blocks, improves test taking, increase your desire for sex. You can use it to overcome a variety of fears and phobias, eliminate allergies, clear up brain fog, break free of limiting beliefs, eliminate anxiety, undesirable thoughts or feelings, neutralize food and addictive cravings, PMS, depression, stiffness or soreness.

As I describe in my book and teach my clients, by using it as I do, you can create kick-butt confidence and overcome a fat and ugly, negative self-image, years of self-doubt, a chronic negative mindset, and so much more. As a professional certified empowerment coach, I love EFT. I consider it the bees' knees of coaching tools and the single best thing that ever happened in my life.

Features of EFT

1. Fast acting: EFT often works rapidly.

2. Painless: It is relatively painless. In the case of dealing with negative memories, you do not have to relive them and re-experience the original trauma.

3 Emotional results are typically long lasting

4. Physical results: vary in lasting ability, (new aspects that need to be dealt with separately can arise.)

5. Specificity: It's best to work on specific events. It makes it easier to tune into the source of the problem.

6. Simple: EFT is an easy, process that you can do yourself. Tap your cares away.

EFT AND WEIGHT - HOW EFT CAN HELP WITH WEIGHT LOSS BY MANAGING FOOD CRAVINGS

We have been told forever that exercise and proper nutrition is the secret path to weight loss. Have you tried to change your diet? Have you done so successfully? Are you exercising all the time? Do you get plenty of rest, limit your alcohol, caffeine and sugar intake, drink lots of water, only to find that ... you are still overweight?!

If this sounds all too familiar, you're not alone.

Tens of millions, possibly hundreds of millions, of people suffering from overweight and obesity have tried very hard to change their situation. This is not a case of an inability to stick to a program or follow a diet. No one wants to be slim, trim, sexy and healthy more than someone who has battled with overweight or obesity for years.

The problem is that the underlying cause for the weight problem has not been addressed.

EFT balances your energy. It lets your energy flow properly through your body once again. There are no blockages which cause physical health problems. The physical process of tapping on energy superhighways makes sure that your energy flow is healthy.

However, there is an emotional side to tapping as well. The affirmation statements you repeat help you heal your emotional state. This allows you to identify root cause emotions and belief systems that are keeping you overweight, even in the face of your best efforts.

You swap that negative belief for a healthy, positive emotion and belief system. You continue tapping to direct healthy energy throughout your body. This provides physical and mental support that can help you finally lose that extra weight, keep it off, and feel great about yourself every step of the way.

Do you find cookies irresistible? Or maybe it's pizza? Or ice cream? If you prefer not to be at the mercy of the siren calls of food, read on to discover how EFT can help.

Imagine this...

You're driving down the street, and the scent of freshly baked pizza hits your nostrils, setting off a bout of cravings. or maybe you're driving past a Krispy Kreme donut store and the red light is on, announcing that they've got a batch straight from the fryer.

What do you do? Make a U-turn and get some?

Or do you struggle with that craving, resist it for the moment, but later eat everything in sight to make up for the deprivation you're feeling?

How about some EFT instead...

EFT, also known as Emotional Freedom Technique is a very powerful mind-body tool that can help with a wide variety of issues. It's especially useful for taming intense negative emotions, and both food cravings and that sense of deprivation if they're (temporarily) resisted qualify. How would you like to be able to tap away those cravings in just a few minutes? Here's how to do it:

1) First, determine the intensity of your negative emotion

Since you're going to experiment, why not try to gauge just how intense that food craving is before you get started. On a scale from 1 to 10, with 1 being complete indifference and 10 being a craving so intense it's practically physically painful, where would you score your current craving. Don't have a current craving? Just do it next time you have one...

2) Next, do the three main parts: The set-up, the actual tapping, and the breath

For the first phase, the set-up, you tap with two fingers of one hand on the karate chop point of the other hand.

3) Here's the set-up, with a possible set-up phrase you could use:

"Even though I feel this craving for...., I choose to feel calm and confident." Repeat this or a similar statement three times, and then move on to the tapping sequence.

4) You start tapping on a series of points with the negative statement

You start tapping on a series of points (see an EFT resource for specifics) and repeat the negative phrase (or variations). For example, you could say, "This Craving," "This craving for pizza," "I really want that pizza," etc.

5) Then, you do a round or two with a positive statement

For example, you could say, "I choose to feel calm and confident," or "I choose to prefer being slim and healthy," or "I value my body more than the pizza."

6) Then, take a deep breath and check how you feel

Now, repeat the gauging of the intensity of your craving. If it's very low, you're done. If it isn't as low as you'd like, do another round of EFT tapping, with the addition of saying "Even though I STILL have some REMAINING craving for pizza..."

EFT FOR EMOTIONAL EFFECTS OF CANCER TREATMENT

Millions suffer from the life-robbing disease that is cancer. There are dozens of types of cancer, and they strike down the young and the old, people from all walks of life, even those who appear otherwise very healthy.

Doctors and other health care providers that treat cancer patients agree that reducing stress is crucial to fighting cancer. Stress and inflammation are closely linked and feed off of each other. Inflammation in your body, especially at the cancerous site, doesn't give you the health needed to fight cancer.

There are also emotional problems that cancer patients have to deal with. They feel limited, incomplete, extremely dependent on others, and in some cases suicidal. This psychological side of cancer is important to understand since we have known since the late 21st century that chronic stress can lead to damage of your DNA.

This not only causes every cell in your body to suffer physically, but it severely reduces the power of your immune system to fight unhealthy invaders like cancer. It makes your cells much more susceptible to becoming cancerous.

EFT works because it is based on the foundation that good health relies on the proper flow of energy throughout your body. Anything that interrupts that flow and blocks your energy leads to stress. As mentioned above, reduce stress, and fighting cancer and its symptoms are easier than if you were in a stressful state. Tapping as a complementary and alternative cancer treatment helps cancer patients deal with the emotional side of their condition, also offering stress relief.

Finding out you have cancer is immediately overwhelming. Fortunately, with good doctors, there's an ever-increasing chance that you will survive and thrive physically for years to come. But the emotional overwhelm can stay with you for a long time because a diagnosis of cancer brings up the specter of death, which is a traumatic experience. The huge emotions that arise create a charge in the nervous system. Along with physical treatment, a method called EFT (Emotional Freedom Techniques) can help alleviate the nervous system charge and calm down the fear, anger, and grief that often result following a cancer diagnosis.

What is EFT?

EFT, also called EFT Tapping, is an "energy psychology" whose basis is similar to that of acupuncture-that there are meridians in our bodies through which energy flows. When everything is fine, the energy is flowing freely, but when we're ill or in pain, something has short-circuited the energy system. In addition to physical pain and illness, as part of this short-circuiting, we often experience painful emotions such as grief, fear, anger, depression, symptoms of PTSD and trauma, phobias, etc.

Trauma can be caused by injuries to your body, such as accidents, falls, assaults, physical abuse-and surgeries. Or it can be caused by emotionally painful events, such as the emotional effects of a cancer diagnosis and the pain and stress of various tests and treatments.

In most cases, EFT Tapping is very effective in alleviating the emotional effects of a cancer diagnosis, the stress of treatments and the emotional after-effects of surgeries by helping the various emotions move through the body and nervous system surprisingly quickly.

Emotional Effects of a Cancer Diagnosis

The first thing that happens when you hear you have any level of cancer, even the very beginnings, is that you automatically feel stressed or traumatized. Right at the beginning of treatment, even before anything else happens, it's traumatic because it's a shock. There's a feeling of urgency and a feeling of unreality. A feeling of wanting to escape out of your body and a feeling of being trapped. Your nervous system veers between high stress and the numbness or spaced out feelings of trauma. To move this trauma through the nervous system, EFT Tapping can often work quite quickly.

Emotional Effects of Cancer Treatment

Procedures following cancer diagnoses can include various kinds of scans and biopsies, chemotherapy and radiation. One of the things that make tests and treatments so stressful is that, for many people, they have no idea what the experience will entail-will it hurt, how long will it take, will they be alone with medical personnel who are strangers and more. If a test or procedure does hurt, or if other complications arise, it can create fear, which can stay in the body and nervous system long after the event is over. Since stress and trauma accumulate in the body, it's good to have a way to clear them out.

Trauma of Surgery

Even though surgery is often one of the main parts of healing cancer, and so, in many ways, it's a relief, the body often (or usually) experiences it as a trauma. The body can experience it as an invasion and it feels helpless due to the anesthesia. In addition, we are unconscious during surgery, which means we're not aware consciously of what is occurring. The trauma, therefore, often stays under the surface and later can affect how we react to stressful experiences in general.

EFT AND YOGA – PERFECT PARTNERS?

Your mind and body are definitely connected. Heal one, and you help heal the other. Work on one, and the other improves. If you have ever exercised or meditated, you no doubt have experienced emotional feelings of health and well-being.

This is because your system rewards positive behavior. Exercise is good for you. Meditation is good for you. As a result, when you engage in these healthy practices, "feel good" hormones are released. This boosts your emotions, making you want to exercise and/or meditate again.

This same connection applies to EFT and yoga.

If you have ever practiced yoga on a consistent basis, you have probably experienced an emotional release at one time or another. It may have come across you and caught you totally unaware. This is because of the connection of your mind, body, and spirit that yoga helps strengthen in a healthy way.

However, a poor emotional state can make your yoga practice suffer. EFT is perfect for resolving stored emotions. Think of tapping as a form of emotional acupressure. You free your negative emotions boosts your positive life force energy, and this, in turn, allows you to experience the spiritual and emotional, physical and mental rewards of yoga to the greatest degree.

EFT makes your yoga practice stronger. Yoga helps prepare your mind and body for EFT. The two practices combined work wonders for a number of emotional and physiological health issues.

Find Emotional Freedom by Combining Yoga and EFT

Have you ever become emotional while practicing yoga? Most likely you uncovered an emotion that was stored deep within the tissues of your body. The body often stores emotions related to situations we have not fully resolved, and some unfinished business remains.

The links between the body and the emotions are not always obvious, but the physical discipline of yoga can help us tune into emotional aspects as well as physical blockages. And when negative, painful emotions arise on the yoga mat, rather than ignoring them, we have another opportunity to release them by exploring the questions "What are our emotions telling us?" and "What do we do about them?

One way to resolve stored emotions is through the Emotional Freedom Technique (EFT), which acts as a form of acupressure for emotional release. The technique was founded by Gary Craig, a Stanford University engineering graduate who set out to find an effective approach to treating emotional issues. The miracle of the Emotional Freedom Technique is that it resolves physical and emotional issues rapidly and permanently.

The premise behind EFT is this: The cause of all negative emotions is a disruption in the body's energy system. On a practical level, what this means is that an event happens, the energy of the body is interrupted, and a negative emotion results. For example, a person witnesses a car accident, the nervous system experiences a jolt, and the response is fear. Someone else may witness the same event without fear. What's the difference? The energetic interruption. This explains why two people can grow up in the same dysfunctional household, and one emerges well-adjusted while the other emerges burdened by negative emotions. The difference has nothing to do with experience. The emotions are caused by the body's energetic response to events and the body's inability to release this negative energy.

Because EFT corrects the body's energetic imbalance, it works equally well no matter what the magnitude of the issue or the emotional attachment. It is effective in treating depression, obsessive-compulsive disorder (OCD), anxiety, guilt, anger, posttraumatic stress disorder (PTSD), addiction, grief, loneliness, and other emotions. The Emotional Freedom Technique was established on the same foundational ground as the Chinese systems of acupressure and acupuncture. The theory behind all of these techniques is that there exist energetic meridians throughout the body. When energy is blocked in the body, it must be unblocked to achieve proper energetic flow. EFT employs a tapping technique that calls for us to tap near the endpoints of the body's energy meridians. Release occurs and negative emotions vanish.

The EFT three-step formula

Although you can read The EFT Manual by Gary Craig and visit various Web sites to view the techniques, you can practice EFT successfully just by following the instructions here. Although there are various levels of complexity with EFT sequencing, the following is a simple but effective version of EFT that works according to the following three-step process: 1) the setup, 2) the sequence, and 3) repeat the sequence.

The setup - Focus on emotion (or situation or concern) you would like to resolve. With the fingertips, on one hand, tap on the side of the other hand (the "karate chop point") while repeating the following neutralizing affirmation: "Even though I feel [insert your emotion, issue, or concern], I deeply and completely love and accept myself." For example, if you are struggling with deep-seated anxiety about your job, you would say, "Even though I have this anxiety about my job, I deeply and completely love and accept myself."

Tap the karate chop point continuously while repeating the EFT affirmation three times out loud and focusing upon the problem or emotion.

The sequence - After the setup, begin the tapping sequence while continuing to repeat the affirmation. The tapping sequence is designed to unblock stuck energy from the body and release it. Tap on the following points (five to seven seconds on each point--roughly the time it will take to repeat your affirmation) in the order listed. Use gentle pressure, not to the point of pain. I suggest tapping both sides of the body with one hand on each side to achieve maximum effect.

EB - Eyebrow

SE - Side of the Eye

UE - Under the Eye

UN - Under the Nose

CH - Chin

CB - Collarbone

UA - Underarm

CR - Crown of the Head

Repeat the sequence - Repeat the tapping sequence, from top to bottom, while repeating the reminder phrase.

Combining yoga and EFT

When combining yoga with EFT, the goal is to excavate the emotions buried within our bodies through various yoga poses to access stored negative emotions and then to use EFT to let go of the energetic disruptions that cause these emotions. The results are profoundly healing.

The effectiveness of the emotional release is greater when the emotions are uncovered at the level of the body rather than the level of the mind. Questioning our minds about our negative emotions is often futile, but when we begin to question our bodies, real answers can emerge, and we can tap out the energetic unbalances that cause our negative emotions. Therein lies the genius behind this approach: it operates at the level of the body to both diagnose and treat.

Yoga and EFT sequence for treating fear

One of our basic fears is the fear of failure, which is essentially a fear of falling. The best poses for eliciting this feeling within us are balancing poses. While performing these poses, focus on your feelings of failure. Hold each yoga pose for three to five breaths.

- Begin by standing in mountain pose. Focus on your breath, on finding your equilibrium. Close your eyes and allow yourself to tune in to your body and to reflect upon your feelings of fear.
- Open your eyes, shift your weight to your left leg, and place the sole of your right foot against the inner left thigh. Stand in tree pose.
- Still standing on the left leg, lift the left arm against the left ear, take hold of the right ankle with the right hand, and hinge forward into dancer's pose, lifting the right leg up behind you. Focus on the feeling of failure in your life.
- When you are at your edge, fold forward and bring both hands to the floor, in a standing split, with the left leg supporting your body and the right leg reaching toward the ceiling. Focus on the feeling of relief that comes with catching yourself when you fall and on the fear of the transition from balancing to falling, to folding into the experience and surrendering to it.
- Transition into half moon pose. Keep your left hand on the floor about a foot in front of your left leg. Rotate

your right leg (which is already lifted) so the inner thigh is parallel to the floor. Place your right hand on your right hip or, if you are confident with your balance, extend the right arm toward the ceiling, and slowly turn your head to look up at the right hand.

- Return to mountain pose. Tuning in to the feelings that arose within your body while doing this sequence, ask yourself: What am I afraid of? Your answer to this question will be the focus of your EFT. For example, if the fear that arises is a fear of not being loveable, you will tap the karate chop point while saying out loud three times, "Even though I have this fear of not being loveable, I deeply and completely accept myself."

- Perform the EFT steps given above (the setup, the sequence, and the repeated sequence).

- Perform this entire balance sequence balancing on the right leg. While doing the sequence the second time, ask yourself what else you are afraid of. When finished with the yoga postures, tap out that fear.

You can do EFT any time, after yoga practice or by itself, running through the sequence in a few minutes and rebalancing your body's energy system in as little as one or two rounds of EFT. You'll be amazed by the results!

EFT FOR LABOR AND BIRTH - 4 WAYS TO GET BETTER RESULTS WHEN USING EFT TO PREPARE FOR YOUR DELIVERY

Unresolved emotional issues can contribute to anxiousness during pregnancy and complications during labor. Users of Emotional Freedom Technique, known most commonly as EFT, already know what a wonderful tool it is for neutralizing negative emotions and fears. EFT's ability to alleviate physical discomfort while simultaneously relieving frustration, and promoting healthy relaxation, makes it a wonderful tool to use during pregnancy and in preparation for birth.

Using EFT To Address Labor Fears

If you are pregnant and feeling apprehensive about labor - simply address your feelings while tapping. To use EFT to address the anxiousness you feel when you think about going into labor, repeat the following while you tap on the Karate Chop Point: "Even though I am afraid of going into labor, I completely and deeply love and accept myself." To help you focus while you tap on the rest of the points repeat a shortened version of that same phrase, something like "This fear of going into labor."

Getting Good Results

Typically, EFT works best when we can be as specific as possible, whenever possible. To increase our chances of getting great results when using EFT to help release a common issue, like the fear of going into labor, it is important that we tap on only one specific issue at a time. It is also important to continuously re-focus your thoughts during the natural reflection points in between rounds of EFT tapping. It can be helpful to use the following four 4 techniques when identifying your issue, and deciding exactly what to tap on:

1) Becoming Aware of Your Body

2) Addressing Specific Events

3) Address Specific Aspects

4) Inner Imagery

When we are working with a large or global issue, like "fear of going into labor" for example, we may be trying to focus on too many feelings at once and EFT may not have any noticeable effect. To tackle such a global issue it is very important to focus in on specific parts of the issue. It is usually very useful to use all four of the following ways of "Getting Specific" as you work through any complicated issue.

Getting Specific with EFT

1. Becoming Aware of Your Body

Where do you feel the feeling in your body? What is it like physically? How do you experience this emotion in your body? For instance:

"Even though I feel the fear like a void in my chest... "

"Even though my throat feels constricted because everyone is always criticizing me... "

"Even though I feel this awful nervousness in the pit of my stomach... "

Many times, after tapping you will feel changes in the way the body is holding the emotion.

The sensations may decrease, change in quality, or even move to a different place in or on your body. When emotional energy moves around the body, this is known as "chasing the pain," and this is a sign that you are on the right track.

2. Specific Events

Break your issue down by focusing in on specific events in your life that made you feel the same way earlier in your life, either recently or in when you were younger. What you believe about labor, birthing, and your body's ability, is based on specific old events, conversations, t.v. shows, etc... As you use EFT to address these specific events and memories as they rise up during tapping, your beliefs about yourself and your expectations of the birth process begin to shift. When addressing specific events with EFT you may say things like:

"Even though my mother told me that giving birth to me was the most terrible thing she ever endured... "

"Even though the woman in labor on the TV show died while giving birth... "

"Even though my doctor told me giving birth naturally would be impossible... "

As you deal with specific events, you will probably start to feel the emotions of those times. By thoroughly tapping for all the details of the memories that feel upsetting, you will effectively erase the discomfort that comes with the larger issue you initially chose to work on. Working with specific events is highly recommended and often gets the most noticeable results. Address each detail of your specific memory with as many rounds of tapping as needed - until your emotional intensity is a 1 or 0. Address each of your feelings, and each of the limiting beliefs you took on, with its very own series of tapping rounds.

3. Address Specific "Aspects"

Every issue we work on has many parts, many details, and many possible triggers for the uncomfortable emotion that we are feeling. Recognizing aspects and tapping very specifically for different aspects is another skill required for effective EFT. For instance, if you are afraid of going into labor, you may have many aspects of that issue to tap on:

- Anticipating the pain of your contractions

- Panicking at the thought of your baby "getting stuck"

- The fear that something unexpected may happen to you or your baby

You can continue to uncover aspects with the question, "What bothers me the most about going into labor when I think about now?" Eventually, there will not be much that bothers you and the fear will be gone, unless there are core issues around which "fear of going into labor" might just be the tip of the iceberg. Many issues carry a complicated mix of emotions. Let's say you have tapped for your hurt in a certain situation. The hurt has subsided, but now you feel angry. As hidden layers of emotion emerge, these are more aspects of the issue and must be handled separately. Looking for different aspects and then specifically targeting these aspects with tapping will go a long way towards achieving lasting results.

4. Inner Imagery

Use an image to give your feeling more detail. If you are good at visualizing, imagine what the energy of the fear looks like, or feels like for you, and tap on the details of that image. Imagery is another way to listen to our feelings. As we tap, images often begin to change as our energy shifts. After tapping, ask yourself has the image changed in any way? How does it feel now? For example:

"Even though this anger is like a big, red ball in the pit of my stomach... "

"Even though this fear is choking me like a snake wrapped around me tightly...

"Even though I feel the sadness like a wave drowning me... "

Change Your Expectations, Change Your Birth Experience

Sit reflectively for a moment after each round of tapping and see what comes to mind. Clues about core issues or events can come up spontaneously as you work on an issue. Just follow your feelings and keep tapping until you feel your emotions becoming less intense.

Using EFT on a daily basis can help you accept yourself as you change and grow in preparation for birth without feeling fear, guilt, anger, resentment or panic. Changing your expectations and your beliefs by letting go of fear and tensions will allow you to birth comfortably. If in doubt contact a qualified professional.

LOW PLATELETS - CAN EFT HELP ITP AND BOOST LOW BLOOD PLATELETS?

Low platelets can be a very serious problem, especially in those diagnosed with an immune system disorder such as Idiopathic Thrombocytopenic Purpura or Lupus.

If you have ITP and low platelets and are fed up with all the conventional medical treatments and are desperately seeking an alternative method of healing your ITP...Listen up! Perhaps it is time to consider EFT.

And just what is EFT you ask? EFT is short for Emotional Freedom Technique, and it appears to combine the foundations of energy medicine, psychology and the principles of acupuncture.

Simply put in the words of EFT's founder Gary Craig, he describes it as such: "EFT is a powerful new discovery that combines two well-established sciences so you can benefit from both at the same time:

1. Mind-Body Medicine

2. Acupuncture (this new version does not require needles-- anyone can do it).

There is voluminous scientific evidence that each of these methods, applied by themselves, can provide impressive relief. But when you combine them both with EFT, a profound synergistic effect is possible. I have observed this repeatedly since 1997 and have seen many stunning results. I believe it is this synergism that allows EFT to sometimes work where nothing else will."

EFT has been developed and used very successfully for a myriad of problems from severe health conditions to emotional and financial problems. To some, it might seem just a little weird and out there, and it's certainly hard to believe that it could actually work, but amazingly enough, it does work. Thousands and thousands will testify as to the effectiveness of this process.

If you have low platelets and are at the end of your rope you might want to read further. There have recently been a couple of documented cases where an EFT practitioner from India has had great success with raising low platelets and could have enormous and far-reaching benefits for low platelet sufferers. In both cases, the ITP victims suffered from Dengue Fever but that doesn't mean that the process would not work for those who have ITP from unidentified causes.

In the first, case this practitioner had a friend who suffered from a severe near-death case of Dengue fever and was on the verge on multiple organ failure. His liver and pancreas were swollen and there was water retention in his lungs and abdomen. His blood count was life-threateningly low.

She went to the hospital to visit him and the situation was very grave. It was definitely a wait and see what happens next event. While waiting, she decided to perform some rounds of EFT on her dear friend. Because he was way too weak to practice the EFT tapping on himself, the EFT practitioner tapped surrogate on herself, on his behalf. Amazingly enough, after a couple of hours of tapping, the client was strong enough to ask her to tap on him, (being her friend, he was already familiar with how EFT was performed. By 8 pm that evening the hospital performed another blood test and miraculously the man's blood count had risen to 106,000. All within a few hours of consistent tapping, (combined with creative EFT approaches).

During this time there was no platelet/plasma administered to him either externally or through IV. The doctors, in this case, were also unaware of her EFT tapping on behalf of her ill friend. In order to explain her friend's amazing recovery, they simply said that he must have unexpectedly responded to their treatments. During the course of his stay, she continued to do consistent rounds of tapping with him. He went back to work a couple of weeks later with a platelet count of 250,000.

Another month later, this same Indian EFT practitioner had another successful experience with helping another person overcome low platelets as a result of their battle with Dengue fever. This person took a little longer to raise their count because they had no prior experience with the process, but their low platelet count definitely came up.

This news could be enormous for those who suffer from low platelets. As there is not much documentation available regarding ITP and the use of EFT to build up low platelets this just may be the beginning of a new cutting edge, non-invasive treatment. I believe that the use of EFT can have far-reaching applications in treating blood count disorders as well as many other problems. EFT is a safe and very effective means of healing, why not try it. Be persistent. It might just work for you. So far nothing else has. What have you got to lose?

IS MTT THE SAME THING AS EFT?

Emotional Freedom Techniques (EFT) are sometimes called Tapping Therapy. Meridian Tapping Techniques (MTT) is sometimes a phrase used interchangeably with EFT. While these powerful, natural healing methods are very closely related, they are not the same.

MTT is a phrase which incorporates all emotional healing techniques that use a certain tapping sequence on acupuncture points throughout the body. In practices like Thought Field Therapy (TFT), "muscle testing" is part of the treatment. This helps to gauge the level of unconscious resistance of the patient.

EFT does not use muscle testing. Gary Craig, credited with founding the current practice of EFT, was concerned that gauging resistance through muscle testing was "loaded for potential inaccuracy" by EFT practitioners without proper training or much experience.

In some ways, EFT can be considered to be a subset of MTT. MTT is a broader term that incorporates all therapeutic approaches in Energy Psychology that involve tapping on acupuncture points on the body's energy meridians. MTT includes standard EFT as well as variations and extensions to EFT. Some variations are different enough from EFT that it was felt that a new term was needed.

A couple of the variations/extensions to EFT include the Choices Method and Matrix Reimprinting. Please note that it is possible that some future MTT methods may deviate so much from EFT, that they should be considered very separate techniques that just happen to have tapped on acupuncture points in common with EFT.

3 Mistakes People Make With EFT and How to Remedy Them

Mistake #1: Fear of Making Mistakes

Placing too much emphasis on "perfection" draws attention away from the real issue we wish to resolve when tapping. To really maximize the benefits, it is best to remain focused on the feeling, the challenge, the issue or the pain while performing the tapping sequence.

What to do: Let go of the need to perform perfectly and just give it a go. Tap with another person or listen to a relevant audio script or find an available video and tap along with it. Another idea is to follow your intuition as your personal guide and find our own tapping sequences. The process is wide open to those of us who want to develop a feel for the process. The bottom line is to find out what works best for you. You may be very surprised by your results.

Mistake #2: Being Too Specific

In many ways, the tapping sequence for a particular topic (for example, fear of public speaking) is like a large tree. Addressing individual events that contribute to that fear (being ridiculed in school or criticized in making a report, for example) might represent the branches of the tree. The trunk of the tree, however, may represent something more fundamental like a failure of basic trust established in very early childhood. Trying to take down the entire tree by attacking the branches can be useful, but potentially disappointing unless one recognizes that the branches need to be followed down to the bottom of the tree. Sometimes issues hide in the symptoms and are more global than we suspect.

What to do: Make a list of the topics or issues you want to address and then look for groupings. These groupings may suggest more global concerns you will want to address.

Sometimes it is useful to have someone you trust help you at this point because it is easy to mistake a branch for a tree. Next, try one or both of the following strategies.

Take the items in each grouping and tap your way through them until you feel that each item has been resolved. If you get stuck on one, go to another, and then go back later and see if the item you skipped still has a "charge." If it does, tap on it again.

Or, treat the grouping itself as an item and tap on it as a whole.

For example, think of a time when you felt afraid to get up and speak before a group. List specific aspects of the experience that upset you (they mistook you for someone else; they forgot to introduce you, etc.). Be very specific and address each of these issues until they no longer bother you. If you still feel the basic fear of getting up to speak before a group, then address the feeling directly and tap on it.

Mistake #3: Feeling Overwhelmed

Sometimes we want to address an issue, but feel overwhelmed and do not know where to start. This can be discouraging and some people will make the mistake of thinking tapping cannot help or that it is too much trouble. Choosing a topic or defining an issue can be very difficult when we are feeling overwhelmed.

For example, we often cling to our long "cherished" responses to various types of events even when we know we will not like the outcome. It is a pattern and we get some kind of "pay off" by reacting in a particular fashion or by simply letting an emotion act itself out And though this may be the best time to act on an issue with tapping, it is also the hardest time to follow through.

What to do: Go find a quiet spot, take a few deep breaths to get centered, and make yourself as comfortable as you can. Focus on breathing deeply and allowing your body to settle in. Take it a step at a time. You may want to relax your body from toes to head, in sequence. Then begin by tapping on the feeling of being overwhelmed. This again can help you to find your focus. Finally, address the upset or the overwhelming issue. Tapping fosters our adaptation to the overwhelming events of all types and we learn how to handle ourselves better in overwhelming situations. Finally, let me offer you a complimentary EFT tap along audio and see if it helps you develop a deeper appreciation for the EFT process.

NEW YEARS RESOLUTIONS, 5 TIPS ON HOW TO KEEP THEM USING EFT

If you're like many, New Years is a time for making resolutions, it's a time when we revisit the past and make new plans for the coming year but how many actually keep them? In this chapter, I'm going to focus on 5 EFT tips (Emotional Freedom Technique) that will help you in keeping your resolutions.

Research has shown that, after six months, fewer than half the people who make New Year's resolutions have stuck with them, and, after a year, that number declines to around ten percent.

With odds like those EFT, tips might come in handy right about now! For many newcomers to EFT knowing what set up phrase to use seems to be confusing so for those that are committed to being successful using EFT the first thing is clarity. Whatever your resolution for the New Year may be it's generally a behavior that we are looking to change or alter, behaviors have underlying emotional issues attached to them so whether your resolution is to stop smoking, go on a diet, exercise more, become financially independent, or address a health issue they all have a common thread and that is the underlying emotions that are driving the behavior.

Gary Craig founder of Emotional freedom technique always emphasizes having a clear picture of what the issue at hand is so in setting up your phrase it is important to be clear and concise, for example, if you're dealing with a childhood issue you would use a setup phrase such as

"Even though when I was five years old my father scared me when he scolded me and told me not to play with my food. I love and accept myself anyway." As opposed to a more global approach such as Even though I'm scared of my father.......

EFT Tip #1 is to be clear on what the issue is

So whatever it is that you wish to accomplish with your New Years Resolution the first step in any journey is always being clear of where you're headed.EFT tips can only be of help if you allow it to work for you and in doing so it is necessary to acknowledge the underlying emotions that may be contributing to the old behaviors. Let's just take exercising more as an example it is a common resolution for many, come January everyone is hitting the gym, buying new equipment, or going on diets but just like any other resolution unless the underlying emotions are addressed your setting yourself up for failure.

EFT Tip #2 Dig deeper

As in the example used above of wanting to exercise more when using EFT you have to get to the core of the behavior using a setup phrase that is too global such as Even though I want to exercise more and I haven't done so........Is not going to get you the results you're looking for. Dig deeper ask yourself why haven't' I exercised more? Allow your subconscious to bring up the answers for you if you go into a place of stillness and ask you will receive an answer! So a more precise setup phrase for this issue would be something like "Even though I overeat because it calms my anxiety and not exercising is just a way of sabotaging my self, I deeply and completely accept myself."

You get the picture; it's about customizing the setup phrase to your personal issues and in order to do so you need to dig a little deeper! If you feel you're stuck and you're not making progress perhaps the use of a trained practitioner would be the best for you, either way, making a commitment is essentially sending a signal to your subconscious mind that you are ready to make that change. Don't be hard on your self Rome wasn't built in a day just because you made a decision doesn't mean you may not come up against an obstacle, but it's not the obstacle but rather how you deal with them.

EFT tip #3 The Movie Technique

If you're still finding it hard to correlate key phrases that you feel are precise to your issue then a visualization technique which is similar to watching a movie might be the key for you. When Gary Craig taught his students EFT often he found that by allowing a client to bring up the memory of the underlying issue that it had a more powerful effect for some especially in cases where individuals had trouble verbalizing. In this technique, you are asked to visualize an actual occurrence or issue as if you were watching it on a movie screen and while doing so do the EFT tapping routine.

Many of us do this automatically and in most cases we may not be consciously aware that we are going back into that time and place much like when an individual is suffering Post Traumatic Stress Disorder and they have flashbacks of a certain trauma that occurred, for many, the trigger takes them back instantly which in turn triggers an emotion and behavior for some it may be difficult to connect the dots and a trained practitioner is advised.

EFT Tip #4 Be Persistent

Persistence, persistence, persistence. This is a point well worth repeating over and over, not all cases experience immediate results but we live in a society that is so used to quick fixes that we are all searching for rapid relief and the miracle cure thereby leading many to give up too soon! Whatever your resolution is for 2011 if there is one thing you should take with you from this article is BE PERSISTENT!

EFT Tip #5 Borrowing Benefits

A Borrowing Benefits group centers on an individual session conducted by an experienced EFT Practitioner. The rest of the participants then tap along according to a detailed set of instructions. Today there are many Meet-up groups that are offering borrowing benefits sessions, led by an experienced practitioner this offers many the benefits of being in a group session and yet have a low cost for attendance. If you are having trouble sticking to your resolution but are really committed to making real changes in your life and the behaviors that may have had negative impacts in the past a group may just be the thing to keep you on track. Remember persistence, persistence, persistence!

RELATIONSHIP IMPROVEMENT TECHNIQUES - USING EFT TO ENHANCE YOUR RELATIONSHIP

Relationships begin as a matter of awareness, gravity/attraction, and desire/chemistry; but these things soon fade leaving people wondering why they got into this relationship in the first place. Understanding that newness doesn't last, and that chemistry (hormones) soon dissipates, is one of the ways to be prepared for the inevitable changes that challenge most relationships; and the Emotional Freedom Techniques (EFT) is another way. Here's how you can use this quick and easy-to-learn, free technique, to enhance your relationship.

EFT is a simple technique you can learn by downloading one of several free manuals available online, as well as by watching any of a number of free demonstration videos; but the technique isn't necessarily the answer to all of your problems. The key to using EFT successfully is in finding the right problem to work on. With relationship problems, most people believe the problem is with the other person unless they have guilt and shame issues, as well as relationship difficulties. The truth is that the problem isn't really a "problem;" relationship difficulties are the result of our programming and how well our relationship matches what we've been programmed to expect.

When the reality we encounter doesn't match what we want or expect to see, we feel stress; and we feel that we are missing something in our lives or relationships. In reality, nothing is missing; we simply don't know how to process parts of our life and relationship that have somehow become stuck in our experience - often due to fear, resistance, or some other uncomfortable emotion. In other words, most relationships can be dramatically improved by simply removing the obstacles or reasons that we aren't fully experiencing and releasing our life and the events in it. By using EFT, you will be better able to go with the flow and let go of the things keeping your relationship from being the best it can be.

To improve your relationship with EFT, you must learn and use this incredibly simple technique to remove the stress and resistance you feel in and around your relationship. When you do, your relationship will dramatically improve almost immediately. Start by making a list of all the negative thoughts and beliefs you are holding onto about your relationship - include statements and feelings you may have about your own self-esteem, body image issues, fears, worries, grief, and resentment where your relationship or partner is concerned. Then simply apply the technique to each statement, one-at-a-time, until the emotional intensity you initially felt has disappeared.

Here are some statements, or beliefs, that some people clear when they begin using EFT to repair or enhance their relationships:

"I don't think this is going to work."

"I don't think anything can save my marriage."

"My marriage is going downhill fast."

"I don't know what to do about my relationship."

"Nothing can help me."

"I'll never be happy."

"I don't deserve to be happy."

"Happiness in relationships is a myth."

"My marriage has lost its spark."

"I can't get over the past."

These are just a few statements, beliefs, or "programs," you can release by simply thinking about them while applying the simple EFT tapping procedure. By tapping on specific points while repeating these limiting beliefs and ideas, your body is encouraged to release the "stuck" information and allow the return of the normal flow of information, ideas, and creativity in your life and relationships. You can probably imagine how difficult it would be to convince someone that their marriage could improve if they were holding onto beliefs about how their marriage cannot get any better. With EFT, limiting beliefs and negative self-talk is quickly and easily released - leaving you free to experience and enjoy a better, more fulfilling and rewarding relationship.

RUNNERS - GET THE MENTAL EDGE WITH EFT

EFT (Emotional Freedom Techniques) is emotional acupressure. It uses gentle tapping on key meridian points to reduce or eliminate unwanted emotions or physical sensations, replacing them with feelings of comfort. Gary Craig, a personal performance coach, developed EFT based on the work of psychologist Roger Callahan and what had been called Thought Field Therapy. In the mid-1980's Callahan accidentally discovered that tapping on certain acupuncture points could rapidly eliminate anxiety and phobias. In my psychology practice, I use EFT every day to help clients recover from emotional trauma and all kinds of emotional suffering.

Runner's can benefit immensely from the regular use of EFT. You can use it to calm pre-race jitters, apply it during a race to ease the suffering of hard running, and use it after a race to reduce the pain of injury or the disappointment of perceived poor performance. Here's how it is done:

1. Select a problem to work on. For example, let's say you want to reduce pre-race nervousness about next Saturday's 5K, days, or even minutes before the gun goes off.

2. Rate your nervousness on a scale of 0-10, with 10 standing for maximum possible nervousness. Let's say your rating of nervousness is a 9.

3. Tap the fleshy edge of either hand, between the bottom of the little finger and the start of the wrist, the part you'd use to "karate chop" something, with several fingers from the opposite hand, while saying the following: "Even though I'm nervous about next Saturday's 5K" (or "next week's marathon"), I deeply and completely accept myself." Continue tapping on the "karate chop" edge of your hand, repeating that phrase two more times for a total of three repetitions. Tapping this way is called the Setup.

4. Now you are ready to tap points on the face and torso, on either side and with either hand. Gently tap 7-9 times on each of these points while saying, out loud, this Reminder phrase, "5K race nervousness," once at each point: eyebrow near nose, bone on side of eye, bone under eye, under nose, indentation on chin, collar bone where it meets rib cage, under arm along side of body, top of head.

5. After tapping all the points, take a deep breath and close your eyes for a few seconds. Then open eyes and notice your level of discomfort, in this example your level of nervousness about the race. Let's assume that your nervousness decreased from a 9 to 6. Next, you would repeat the Setup using slightly different language.

For the Setup, continuously tap the karate chop edge of either hand, saying, "Even though I still have some of this 5K race nervousness, I deeply and completely accept myself." Repeat two more times. Then, tap all the head and torso points as before, saying once out loud at each point "the remaining 5K race nervousness."

6. Repeat step 5 until the nervousness has decreased to level 2 or below.

You can use an abbreviated version of EFT during a race or hard training. No Setup is required. Simply tap on one or two of the points as you are running, while repeating silently to yourself "this discomfort" or "this heavy breathing" or just simply "RELAX". You can experiment with which point(s) and phrase(s) give you the best results, i.e., the greatest relief from emotional or physical suffering.

To use EFT to reduce bad feelings after a disappointing race, try this formula. First, notice how you feel and measure, from 0-10, how sad, frustrated, or disappointed you are. Use your own word to describe it. Then do the Setup and tapping as with the previous example.

SETUP: Tap the karate chop point continuously, saying out loud, "Even though I missed my goal time (or goal place) and feel disappointed, I deeply and completely accept myself." Repeat two more times. Then tap the head and torso points as described above, using this Reminder phrase "missed my time (or place) disappointment." Take a deep breath, close eyes for a few seconds, and then once again measure the intensity of your feelings.

Assuming the intensity has decreased somewhat, repeat Setup saying three times "Even though I still have some of that 'missed my time disappointment' (or frustration, sadness, or whatever) I deeply and completely accept myself." Then tap the head and torso points, repeating at each point, "the remaining 'missed my time disappointment' " (or sadness, frustration). Take a breath, close eyes for a few seconds, and then measure intensity again. Repeat above sequence, tapping until the remaining intensity is level 2 or below. Notice that the Setup and Reminder phrases do not have to be grammatically correct, but they should refer to a specific issue or event.

Top Reasons to Be Grateful For EFT

Easy To Learn

This has to be one of the things to be most grateful for about EFT. You can learn the basic routine and start applying it immediately. There are so many websites you can read, videos you can watch, free pdf files and the 'big' EFT manual that you can download and read later. You really can learn it and start using it in a matter of minutes. There are also so many excellent practitioners whom you can study and learn with and from too.

Quick To Do

Once you have learned the basic pattern. You can start applying it to any limiting decision, negative emotion, negative belief or just whenever you feel that you have a block which stops you from either getting something or letting something or somebody leaves your life.

EFT Always Works

EFT always works. The basic pattern even gives you a way of scoring to know that it is working for you. When you start using EFT, one of the hardest things is to know, is that it is working for you. A way of recognizing that it is built right into the system. Don't be fooled by EFT's apparent simplicity.

Works When Nothing Else Will

You can use EFT on yourself, by yourself, anytime, anyplace and anywhere. You don't need to tell anybody else what you are doing. You will use EFT when you have tried everything else. When you do, you'll be ready for it. I've had more Champagne moments and quick emotional releases of my negative stuff than anything else I've tried.

Quickest Negative Emotional Release of Everything

Literally within a matter of minutes, I've let go of stuff that I've carried around with me for years and years. Some of it was so well hidden I had no idea, until EFT and I let it go.

YOUR VIBRATION - HOW ABUNDANCE TAPPING CAN CHANGE IT

Do you know you can be more than you are? That your life can be more fulfilling, successful and joyful? Abundance Tapping is one way to change your vibration - and your life.

You are creating your life, in every moment, by the vibration that is emanating from you.

This vibration is generated by the thoughts that you think and the emotions that you feel. Together, they equal your vibration.

Low vibration is caused by negative thinking.

By critical, pessimistic, self-conscious, blaming, scared, "I can't do it, life is hard, it's all their fault," thinking.

The corresponding emotions would be fear, anger, irritation, worry, discouragement, helplessness, hopelessness.

Together, those thoughts and emotions put out a vibration that attracts events, people and circumstances to your life that are likely to evoke the same vibration.

This is how lots of anxious thoughts can attract more anxiety-causing events to your life. The Law of Attraction is Like a Radio Because the universe acts like a radio when you tune your vibrational dial to fear, you get fearful, scary people, things and events in your life.

Now, the question you may be asking is what can you do about this? How can you change your vibration?

Because if you're feeling anxious all the time, to just say, "Quit being anxious. It's a bad vibe and it's gonna bring negative things into your life," doesn't work. In fact, it may cause you to feel even more anxious!

Our habitual thoughts, the beliefs that we hold, and our recurring feelings were mostly initiated by events in our childhoods. Usually in our families or at school.

The events of our lives stimulated us to make meaning out of them. Here's an example. Let's say you drop and break something as a young child, a two-year-old. You look at your mother's face for her reaction. You interpret her facial expression as upset, or disappointed, disgusted or angry.

Like a little toddler, you may decide that look means there is something wrong with you. That you are bad. That you are a bad person.

She doesn't suspect what's going on inside you. She's just thinking about the mess she has to clean up and her frustration.

So you conclude you're defective.

That conclusion is drawn and that is the formation of a belief. A belief you may hold your entire life.

Without being questioned and transformed, that belief can act your whole life to limit you. The belief that there's something wrong with you can limit what you can accomplish and achieve. Or even what you can experience, in terms of joy, love and, of course in the abundance you can attract into your life. And that belief will perpetuate itself.

When you hold the belief there's something wrong with you, you look for evidence that it's true. You interpret more looks to confirm your belief. You think you hear people saying there's something wrong with you. And your vibration brings you more experiences that feel like you're defective. It's a vicious cycle or Catches 22. The lousier you feel, the lousier your life becomes and the lousier you feel.

And here's the bad news.

99.99% of us carry around the belief that there's something wrong with us, that we're defective, unlovable, not good enough.

The result?

Our lives are half lived. We don't rise to our true potential. Our true brilliance is dimmed.

Now, conversely, if you are feeling a sense of power, of joy, of love, of appreciation, of "anything is possible," of confidence and capability, then...

...your vibration, made of your thoughts and emotions, sent out through the universe, will bring back events, circumstances, and people which match that vibration.

So you're much more likely, with good vibration, to attract good opportunities, trustworthy, helpful and loving people, healthy relationships and abundance in all areas of your life. How can we transform those core beliefs? Through decades of reading self-help books, going to workshops and working with professionals in multiple areas of healing, eventually, I stumbled upon the method called Emotional Freedom Techniques.

Of all the dozens of methods that I have learned and used...

...Abundance Tapping is the only one that has enabled me to reliably produce positive results every time I use it, to move me from a lower vibrational state to a positive vibrational state.

EFT goes way beyond positive thinking.

Because it actually acknowledges the dark thoughts, the scared, pessimistic part of us that cannot be permanently cleansed, removed or repressed anyway. And it enables us to move from a negative to a positive state. Why I Love Abundance Tapping Having a technique that I can use myself, to quickly and easily transform my negative thoughts and emotions has been liberating to me.

EFT is not the only method out there that can do this. But it's the best one I've found. It's the best fit for me, of all the techniques I've used.

Abundance tapping may or may not be a good fit for you. You won't know until you do a little study, learn the process and give it a go. That can take you about a week of learning and testing. If you get results, keep learning and doing EFT.

WHY DEVELOPING YOUR EFT NICHE IS SO CRITICAL FOR SUCCESS

Skillful EFT or Tapping practitioners are not necessarily skillful business-persons. Individuals commonly are exposed to tapping through a variety of experiences, often witnessing profound transformation and healings. Those events can be so powerful that they make the choice to devote their lives to EFT and begin a new career, brimming with excitement and passion. If, however, they have no entrepreneurial skills or have never run a business or a private practice before, they can easily become overwhelmed by the need to wear multiple job description hats.

New practitioners may be novices in the technology and marketing skills that are so helpful in growing an EFT practice. There is an endless learning curve for understanding website creation and search engine optimization (SEO), blogging skills, social media marketing, and creating teleclass or online products. Emotional challenges often emerge ranging from anxiety related to charging clients for the first time for services to the fear of public speaking or even the tongue-tying process of describing what you do when someone asks.

When someone asks what you do, what do you say? Do you offer something like "EFT is emotional acupuncture without needles," which leaves them with that quizzical look? Do you do your best to describe acupoint stimulation as reducing amygdala hijacking only to have them say, "That's great," and then change the conversation topic?

I will offer a secret that makes this big question far easier to answer and much more likely to create new clients. It is what we tell our EFT business students from day 1 of their training. When you develop your business niche, your response will become simple and engaging.

Try this experiment: Ask the next 100 strangers you meet: "Do you know what EFT is?" Of course, the response will vary with the demographics of your community. While the recognition is growing by leaps and bounds, my experience is still that under 10% say yes. So when someone asks my friend Jean what he does and he says he is a plumber, 100% nod their head in recognition. I would estimate that there are far fewer taxidermists than there are EFT practitioners, yet many more people will understand the former over the latter. So what is there to do?

Within the polite 20 seconds, you get to respond to the question regarding what you do, you can try to explain or EFT or you can develop your practice niche and respond like this: "What do I do? I help women who have been recently divorced find their confidence and self-worth to create the relationship of their dreams!" Or "I help first-time authors who are stuck move quickly through their writer's block to complete their dream book project!" Or "I'm a coach who works with individuals with dental fears get over their worry so they can feel excited about having healthy teeth again!"

You may notice a few things about this. First, there is no need to form the get-go to explain "the EFT tool." If the person is a good client fit, then he or she will truly be interested in a deeper conversation in which you can offer a more in-depth explanation as to how you would help achieve that goal. Even if the individual is not an ideal client fit, he or she will more than likely immediately think of a distinct person who would be. When you respond to the question by saying that you do EFT, it is unlikely that your listener will think of someone who needs you.

Now you might think, "Oh goodness, why would I want to limit my clients to a limited number of interested potential clients when I am just starting out? Shouldn't I keep my practice open to everyone?" The irony is that by being a generalist to everyone you are a specialist to no one, and that is likely to have your client calendar awfully quiet. Dental fears affect nearly 20% of the population, and in the United States, that's 68 million people. With divorce running around 50% in America... well, you do the math. As heartbreaking as it is, people take action when they are suffering. People will pay for services when they are hurting; that is when they search and ask for help.

You might think, "Do I really only want to work with people with dental fears?" The reality is that the issue that someone complains of is usually only the starting point and you may find yourself working with any number of different issues. In sessions, a client may clear a long-standing fear of dogs after being bitten as a child. That client works at an animal shelter and refers all her coworkers, none of whom have dental fears.

HOW TO HAVE YOUR OWN PERFECT BODY SHAPE, SIZE AND WEIGHT EASILY - IT'S DOWN TO YOU AND EFT

As already mentioned, EFT works on both the psychological and physical levels which thereby create self-love and self-acceptance in the user. This acts as vandalism towards the issues which are barriers to weight loss. Hence through this way it helps to cut cravings, overeating, big eating and other not exercising campaigns. Mostly this follows to the creativity or imagination of the positive inflow of the body.

To lose weight, all you have to do is eat less and exercise more.

Easy, isn't it? So why can't you?

There are many emotional and physical reasons why we put the weight on in the first place. Having said that, many of us that are overweight manage to keep it on for longer than makes sense.

Take my friend Hannah. Well-liked for her hospitality, she feeds you plenty whenever you go to visit. Her kitchen is full of cakes and snacks. Her living room is scattered with chocolates, biscuits, and cookies. She tells you of all the meals she has cooked for her family that week and gives you new recipes that she's found. She's tried them and they're delicious.

Can you imagine if Hannah had been a heroin addict?

Take my friend Hannah the heroin addict. Well-liked for her hospitality, she makes sure she has a good supply whenever you go to visit. Her kitchen is scattered with burnt spoons and discarded bits of aluminum foil. Her living room is full of the sickly-sweet smell of brown. She tells you of how the social services have taken the last remaining child off her that week and give you the number of the new dealer that she's found. She's slept with him and he's given it to her cheap.

Not so homely and cuddly anymore, is she now?

Overeating is an addiction. Many people who overeat also over-exercise. Some both overeat and deliberately under-exercise. And every time I think I have heard all the excuses, I hear another, even more, inventive one. "I'm too fat to expose my body in a swimsuit"; "I have a slow metabolism" said as she tucks into the 17th chocolate bar that day; "Gyms are full of slim, sexy people" [no they're not, and how would you know anyway if you've never been?]; "This isn't bad for you," said about the 14th fast-food snack that day; "I need comfort food"; "This is too good to waste"; etc. But the excuses are not the work of a lazy person or someone with no will-power. Quite the opposite. It takes a lot of hard work and determination to maintain excessive weight.

With EFT, we define those excuses as the work of a psychologically-reversed mind. The mind of someone whose body's "energy" system is against their recovery. EFT or Emotional Freedom Techniques addresses the psychology and the "energy" aspects of the condition at the same time. We use tapping to stimulate acupuncture meridian end-points whilst applying some clever psychology to free us from these excuses and allow us to be happily slim, attractive and healthy again.

EFT can be used as a motivator for your exercise program, removing the emotional blocks that are in the way of your success. It can unravel all those emotional root causes of the comfort eating.

EFT is also a very neat tool that literally changes the taste of foods. What is good for you end up tasting delicious and what is bad for you end up tasting unbearably disgusting. You literally tap the EFT sequence on your face, body, and hands as you repeat a special phrase and look at, smell and taste the food. The food stays the same, only your perception of it changes. Fatty foods taste like petrol jelly. The average chocolate bar tastes of artificial flavorings, wax, hydrogenated vegetable fat, and sickly-sweet sugar. The average bread takes on the strong taste of yeast. Chocolate pudding tastes like hair conditioner. Cookies and cakes are hard to dissolve in your mouth, that is if you can get yourself to put them there. Gradually or all of a sudden, a new phrase that you are saying as you tap on the EFT points changes the smell, taste, and texture of the food. You really have to experience it to appreciate the full effect.

Made in United States
Troutdale, OR
11/03/2024

24266725R00065